D1408647

101 B

Hydra Publishing
Publisher: Sean Moore
Designer: Gus Yoo
Editor: Sarah Litt

First Published in 2002 by BBC Worldwide Ltd,
Woodlands,
80 Wood Lane, London W12 0TT

Edited by Alison Willmott

Commissioning Editor: Nicky Copeland
Project Editor: Sarah Lavelle
Book Design: Claire Wood
Design Manager: Lisa Pettibone
Picture Researcher: Victoria Hall

First American Edition published in 2003
02 03 04 05 10 9 8 7 6 5 4 3 2 1

Published in the United States by
Hydra Publishing
50 Mallard Rise, Irvington,
New York 10533

ISBN 1-59258-008-4

A catalog record for this book is available from the Library of Congress

Set in Amasis MT, ITC Officina Sans,
New Baskerville
Printed and bound in France by Imprimerie
Pollina s.a. - L88862a
Color origination by
Kestrel Digital Colour, Chelmsford

BBC Worldwide would like to thank the following for providing photographs and permission to reproduce copyright material. While every effort has been made to trace and acknowledge all copyright holders, we would like to apologize should there have been any errors or omissions.

All photographs © *BBC Good Homes magazine*, with the exception of: Abode 35, 71, 105, 111, 123, 149, 163, 169, 177, 181, 199; © *BBC Homes & Antiques* 53, 103, 107, 121, 161, 167, 173, 175, 206, 207; CP Hart 17, 63, 109, 113; Dolomite 15, 33; Dolphin 45, 49; Ideal Standard 59, 95, 115, 117, 124, 125, 147, 151, 187, 209; Lu Jeffery 27, 154, 155; Magnet 9, 119; Royal Doulton 19; Sottini 25, 157; Twyford Bathrooms 41.

Distributed by St. Martin's Press

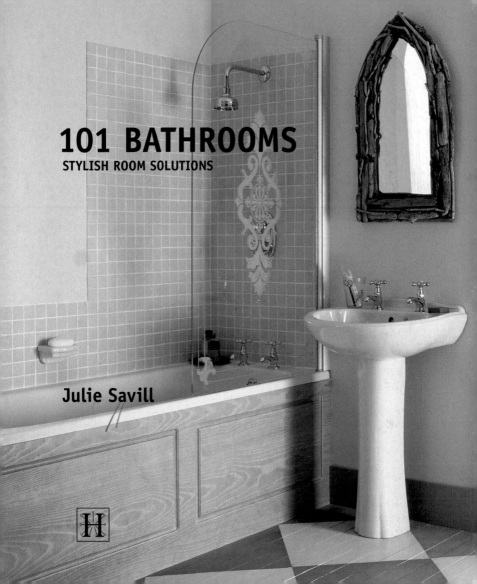

101 BATHROOMS

STYLISH ROOM SOLUTIONS

Julie Savill

CONTENTS

747.78
Sa940

BUDGET 126

CLASSIC 146

CREATIVE 188

7/28/03   9.95

INTRODUCTION

There's something very indulgent and slightly decadent about the thought of going all out for your dream bathroom. But this workhorse room is on duty 24 hours a day, working even harder than the kitchen and used by virtually every visitor to your home – so doesn't it deserve a bit of glamour and stardust?

Your plans for your bathroom are likely to be dictated by space as much as budget. Older properties, originally built with an outside loo, have occasionally sacrificed a bed-room to create a luxuriously large bathing space with, in the most extravagant cases, room for a sofa or chaise longue. But for most of us that is a little fantasy to save for another day while we battle with more recent homes, bathrooms of more petite proportions and all the demands of a busy family.

A white suite is your best friend in the bathroom. It's timeless, looks great with all manner of color schemes and won't put off prospective purchasers if you decide to sell up and move on. Of course, if money is very tight or you are doing a quick fix before putting the place on the market, there are ways to bring a colored suite more up to date – you'll find some ideas in this book. If, on the other hand, you have a little more cash to splash, your first move should be to ditch the avocado or primrose yellow in favor of a little white or palest cream number.

A daring raid on a few bath-room showrooms is your next move. Arm yourself with a whole range of brochures – not only for the bathrooms illustrated, but for the neat little sets of graph paper and cut-out templates for toilets, sinks and bathtubs you'll find at the back. A happy evening spent with scissors and one of these planning kits will let you explore all the possibilities before taking the plunge and ordering your new fittings.

Once you've made your plans and your plumber has the major fittings in place, the really creative stuff starts. Forget wall to wall white tiles – a bathroom is as deserving as any other room in the house of a carefully considered and thoughtfully executed color scheme. Consider how the room is going to be used for the practical elements. If you have young children, water-proof walls and floors are going to be a top priority but don't leave yourself out of the equation. As well as the pure function of keeping everyone clean, the bathroom may be the only room where you can lock the door and be truly alone for half an hour. Make sure it has flexible lighting, plenty of storage to clear the clutter and somewhere to rest a glass of wine. At the end of a hard day, this is your sanc-tuary and you'll thank yourself for the little extras you've managed to plan in…

Julie Savill, Editor
BBC Good Homes magazine

The look: Form and color fall into perfect harmony when lush lilac creates a chic setting for shapely fittings. The sensual curves of the suite offset the geometric wall stripes and the angular lines of the bath surround.

Color: Cool and contemporary, purple and lilac are rich in color but also relaxing to live with, and team beautifully with white and chrome fittings. This calming scheme blends a range of toning shades – from pale lavender floor tiles to deep purple accents. Contrasting wall treatments highlight the room's unusual shape, with light stripes livening up the foreground walls and a more intense lilac creating a cosier feel in the bathing area.

Suite: The suite combines minimalist styling with smooth curves for a contemporary, contoured look that's easy on the eye. The gently rounded shape of the sink is echoed by the close-coupled toilet.

The corner bath also adds attractive shape, giving a more individual look than a standard rectangular design. Sleek chrome taps highlight the suite's modern appeal.

Walls: If you want to add interest to walls without overpowering your room with pattern, paint stripes in two similar shades. Or, for an even subtler effect, alternate gloss and matte emulsion in the same hue, creating a variation in texture. Broad horizontal stripes will make a room feel wider but also appear to lower the ceiling, so are best used in tall rooms.

Floor: Ceramic tiles make a hardwearing bathroom floor and are available in many colors. However, they feel chilly beneath bare feet and can be slippery when wet. You may also find it difficult to keep the grout clean.

CONTEMPORARY

The look: Cool cream paint and tiles the color of milky coffee give this bathroom a tranquil atmosphere, perfect for enjoying a long soak. Tongue-and-groove boarding encloses the bathtub and tank, giving the small space a streamlined look.

Color: If you want to enhance the illusion of space in a small room, pale colors are your best bet. White is an especially effective brightener but can feel stark and chilly; soft cream is much easier to warm to and creates a light but relaxing environment. Using the same shade throughout a room also makes it feel bigger, as it avoids breaking up the wall area with different colors. Cream paint covers both the walls and tongue-and-groove panelling, and coffee-colored tiles in a closely toning shade continue the visual harmony. The wooden flooring and Venetian blind add a hint of warm, natural color to complement and offset the pale neutrals.

Suite: Wall-mounted sinks are available in smaller sizes than pedestal designs but must be fixed to a solid wall that can take the weight of the sink when full of water. Here an H-shaped structure, made from timber and roughly plastered plasterboard, provides additional support. Back-to-wall toilets have a tank that can be concealed behind a false wall or panelling, and boxing this one in with tongue and groove that matches the bath panels gives a neat, uniform look.

Window: A Venetian blind is a versatile treatment for a small or narrow window as its adjustable slats give you complete control over light and privacy levels. Wooden blinds are now widely available, and work well in a contemporary setting.

The look: Orange is a warm, 'advancing' color that creates a welcoming atmosphere. This room intensifies its rich, glowing quality by using toning shades repeatedly in different fittings and materials.

Color: Strong color looks at home in smaller spaces if similar shades are used over most available surfaces. The bathroom is the perfect place to experiment with color from all types of materials, and here copper, brass, lacquered wood and plastic all add a new dimension to the palette of fiery hues. Different textures also affect color – glossy surfaces reflect light, helping to enhance the illusion of space, while brushed or satin finishes provide a contrast for matte walls without the need to add different colors.

Sink: A compact sink fitted into a narrow washstand is a neat solution for a small bathroom, and shelves provide easily accessible storage. The wooden cabinet is dressed to fit the scheme with a covering of thin copper sheeting, available from metal merchants or large DIY stores, which is also used to make a reflective splashback. The matching towel rack is made from 2.2cm copper piping, with elbows at either end. A tall-spout faucet with gleaming brass finish completes the line-up of glamorous metallics.

Bath: Save strong shades for walls and accessories – white fittings are more versatile than colored ones. An edging of triangular ceramic tiles in oxblood red helps to incorporate the bath into the scheme.

Accessories: The yellow stool and brown towels add dashes of accent color that help to offset the hot reds and oranges. The round mirror, complete with candle sconces, enhances the room's cosy, romantic atmosphere.

BATHROOM TIP
Good ventilation is vital in a bathroom, especially if it has no window. An extractor fan fitted to an outside wall will reduce condensation. A fan can be set to come on with the light and continue working for a while after it is switched off

The look: Simple wooden cabinets and elegantly styled fixtures bring Shaker style into the bathroom, with natural textures and traditional accessories bringing out the essence of all-American country charm.

Color: Pale neutrals offset by warm wood tones create a look that's plain but inviting. The richness of the cream used on the units is enhanced by contrast with the white walls and fittings. The natural browns of the woods stand out against the light backdrop and make their presence felt by appearing throughout the room. The horizontal lines of the pegboard and countertop are echoed by the wood-effect laminate flooring.

Suite: In keeping with Shaker principles, the fittings appear stylish but functional, the sink and bath combining distinctive form with generous capacity. The swan-neck faucets have an old-fashioned, utilitarian feel that is also well in character. Some bathroom companies can design and install a combination of fixtures and furniture, so that fittings can be incorporated into your storage system. The back-to-wall toilet has its tank hidden inside the cupboards, and the semi-recessed sink is built into the countertop, allowing space below to be used for plenty of storage.

Storage: Built-in cabinets are the neatest way of maximizing storage capacity, and an L-shaped layout makes efficient use of space. The doors of the base cabinets have classic Shaker styling, with simple recessed panels. Their smart chrome handles echo the taps. The wall cabinet adds further concealed storage. It also has attractive display niches at either side, and doors that double as mirrors. Shaker traditions continue with the pegboard and selection of oval wooden boxes, both hallmarks of the style.

The look: Simple modern fixtures show off their curvaceous lines against a restful backdrop of deep blue and taupe, while accessories add a hint of oriental style to complement this coolly minimalist scheme.

Color: Painting neighboring walls in contrasting colors can add an extra dimension to a room. For a calming effect, choose two shades that are similar in tone. Neutrals are a safe bet as they team well with most other colors, and cool hues such as blue have a more relaxing effect than reds, yellows and oranges. This cool combination is complemented by the warmer natural tones of the wood flooring, and freshened by the white fittings and the pale colors of the painting on the wall.

Suite: The fixtures combine style with practicality, the compact floorstanding toilet featuring a streamlined upright tank and the bowl of the circular sink offering a large capacity without taking up too much space. The chrome-plated monoblock taps with traditional controls would suit either a modern or classic setting.

Glass wall: Glass blocks make ideal partitions for modern bathrooms. As well as having an up-to-the-minute feel, they provide just enough privacy to screen a bath or shower area without blocking out natural light. You can buy them from DIY stores, but it's best to get a professional to lay them as glass walls must be reinforced for safety.

Accessories: The slatted wooden bench, waffle-weave towels and shapely dark vase add a suggestion of oriental minimalism. Every room benefits from a touch of art, and the bathroom is no exception: the painted canvas echoes the wall colors, bringing them together as subtler shades.

BATHROOM TIP
When planning a new bathroom layout, take into account the position of existing plumbing – it can be costly to change. If possible, the toilet and bidet should be placed side by side

The look: Although based on the colors of nature, this is no country-style bathroom. Alluring dark woods and subtle shades of stone create a sophisticated backdrop for modernist fittings. Used as simple blocks of color, they combine minimalist styling with natural warmth.

Color: The palette of restrained neutrals reflects the contrasting light and dark shades found in nature. The pale beige flooring and the grey paintwork on the right-hand wall blend with soft cream and white, while the deeper shades of the stone-colored tiling and dark wood surfaces give the scheme a stronger look. Dark woods suggest oriental or jungle inspiration: to bring out that exotic quality, add accessories in jazzier accent colors, such as bright red and leaf green.

Suite: Clean curves and simple design give the fittings their thoroughly contemporary character. The freestanding bath creates an air of luxury, its oval shape and generous proportions making it the focal point of the room. It is sold complete with the wooden feet that fit in so well with this natural scheme. The chrome taps have gold-plated knobs, a distinctive detail that adds a hint of glamour. They are fitted centrally so that two people can share the tub in comfort.

Accessories: The large mirror that spans the width of the far wall helps to give the room a greater sensation of space. To maintain minimalist purity, there are only a few toiletries and vases on display – these reflect the browns and creams of the scheme. A small slatted stool reinforces the look with further natural texture.

The look: Mix old and new for a bathroom full of color and character. An original roll-top bathtub complements this high-ceilinged Victorian room, but striking color contrasts and slick storage create a look that's right up to date.

Color: Clean up with dazzling white for a bright, modern atmosphere – white flooring and wall tiles are guaranteed to lighten the mood. Teaming them with deep blue forms a dramatic contrast, adding real color impact. Accents of fuchsia pink help to soften the look, and using this color to paint the bath makes it seem at home in the contemporary scheme.

Suite: A traditionally styled bath/shower combo with a chrome finish is in character with the classic roll-top bath. The sink, toilet and bidet have clean, simple lines that suit the modern scheme, but their smooth curves also complement those of the bath.

Storage: With a radiator running along most of one wall, the room had little space for freestanding storage furniture. The solution was a clever system, built by a local carpenter, which fits around and above the radiator and incorporates open shelves, mirrored wall cabinets and a peg rail. Positioning the rail above the radiator ensures that towels hung from it remain warm, aired and dry.

Floor: Many old houses still have original floorboards which, if in good condition, can be painted. Two coats of white floor paint give these boards a hard-wearing finish. Bathroom floors must be sealed with varnish to stop water penetrating the wood.

The look: With billowing curtains and blue-washed walls, this room borrows the colors of a spring sky to create a beautifully refreshing atmosphere. Natural textures and accessories join a varied mix of furniture and fittings to give the look its laid-back, modern charm.

Color: In a room where daylight floods in through a tall window, the pale blue and white scheme guarantees an ultra-bright environment. The checks of the mosaic tiling, shower curtain and cushion cover vary the tone with hints of darker blue, which are reinforced by the ultramarine border painted around the floor. The natural tones and textures of the pine flooring and toilet seat provide a warm contrast for the airy colors.

Walls: Applying paint as a colorwash adds interest to large wall areas, and pale shades create a cloudy, ethereal effect. First apply a base coat of white paint and leave to dry. Then either dilute your top color with water until you get the strength you want, or mix in a little scumble glaze. Working on a small area at a time, use large brush strokes to spread the color over the wall, allowing some of the white base coat to show through.

Suite: The reproduction claw-foot bath fits in well with the room's Victorian features, and the sink has classic lines. Laid-back looks thrive on a mix of styles, so the bath and basin sit happily amid the room's fresh, contemporary decor.

Accessories: A sheer white curtain screens the large window while letting plenty of light filter through. Plants, pebbles and a fiber mat all contribute natural texture, while the Lloyd Loom chair adds both character and comfort.

The look: Modern minimalism demands clutter-free surfaces and clean lines, and this room's fitted units make both possible. The beautifully rounded suite and light but livable color scheme give cutting-edge looks a gentler complexion.

Color: Although white is the most versatile choice for a suite, cream creates a softer look, and is complemented by walls and flooring in a similar shade. The storage units mellow the scheme further with the natural look of wood, but their black countertops add smart definition. The lime green wall also sharpens things up with a dash of fresh, contemporary color.

Suite: The organic shapes of the fittings provide a stylish contrast for the straight lines of the storage units. These practical units keep the room streamlined by concealing the tank and pipes of the back-to-wall toilet, as well as the pipework to the semi-recessed sink. The double-ended bath has a central tap control, a sleek single-lever knob in shiny chrome.

Storage: Bathrooms generate a surprising amount of clutter – toiletries, towels, cleaning materials – much of which is not worth keeping on show. Built-in cabinets look neat and modern, while providing particularly generous storage capacity. A combination of drawers and cupboards takes care of different-sized items, while the countertops and the glass shelves above the sink provide display space for dressier accessories.

Shower stall: If you have the space and resources to build one, a shower stall will provide total privacy for showering. To save space, choose sliding doors or ones that open into the cubicle, as these do not take up additional floor area.

The look: If you haven't space for a bath, look on the bright side – showers use less water, which is reflected in your water bills. An open-plan shower area maintains the illusion of light and space in this narrow room.

Color: While off-white tiles keep the look bright and airy, the overall color palette achieves a relaxing atmosphere, combining soft green with pale neutrals. A few grey tiles and a grey marble shelf on the partition wall add subtle interest to the shower area, while accents of wood and wicker add touches of welcome warmth.

Shower: If you can give your shower enough space, you may not need to enclose it completely, but make sure the surrounding walls have a splashproof covering, such as tiles. Here a low wall protects the toilet and sink from the shower's spray. A shower head on a sliding rail, with a detachable handset, gives greater flexibility than a fixed design. The head can be adjusted to suit people of different heights, or removed from its fitting for hair-washing or cleaning the shower space.

Suite: The smooth curves of the toilet and sink provide a contrast of form with the geometric lines of the shower area and tiling. The toilet is a close-coupled design, which looks neater than a model where the tank and bowl are linked by a connecting pipe.

Accessories: Bath mats are essential in a carpeted room; two large ones catch splashes. A trendy wire basket on the shower wall and a glass shelf above the basin keep washing items handy. The wicker laundry basket and wooden picture frames add a hint of country style to this contemporary scheme.

The look: Create a dazzling contrast with crisp white and brilliant azure blue. The strength of the white fittings against the dark backdrop is the key to this vibrant look.

Color: For maximum effect, be brave with your background color – choose a deep, intense blue and use it to cover the walls. The fittings will sing out against it, but adding a panel of white tiles increases their impact, creating a more equal balance with the blue. Add texture to soften the look, with green mosaic-effect floor tiles and a scattering of mottled lime tiles to break up the plain white splashback. The dark wood and wicker cabinet introduces warmth, and green glass accessories add drama as their color is intensified by the blue walls.

Suite: Fittings with clean, simple designs reinforce the bold modern appeal of the look, offering no fussy details to distract from the color contrast. The chrome faucets also have streamlined contemporary looks, with easy-to-operate taps. The bath is panelled with three strips of MDF, painted with a white satin finish.

Floor: The flooring looks like ceramic tiles but is in fact a high-quality vinyl, which is warmer and softer underfoot. Waterproof and easy to clean, vinyl designs include a wide range of patterns that look just like real stone, wood or ceramics, including these convincing mosaic-effect tiles.

Furniture and accessories: The garden chair and the natural textures of the storage cabinet add character to the look. Rope pots displayed on the simple shelf introduce further woven texture, while the glitzy mosaic border of the mirror echoes the floor tiles.

BATHROOM TIP
Monoblock sink faucets fit into a single hole, leaving more of your sink top free for toiletries or accessories. By enabling you to mix hot water with cold before it leaves the spout, they reduce the risk of scalding

The look: Curvy lines manipulate space in this tiny bathroom, adding interest among the simple styling and understated color scheme, and softening the overall look.

Color: The grey wall tiles are pale enough not to overpower the small space, while providing a tranquil backdrop for the white fixtures. In this super-subtle scheme, the horizontal band of blue provides welcome color interest, and also breaks up the wall area, helping to make the room appear wider.

Walls: A surround built out from the left-hand wall follows the lines of the bath and provides a screen between the shower and sink. Its curvy walls are made from waterproof plywood covered with mosaic tiles, and recesses knocked into the plywood provide useful storage niches. If you've never worked with mosaic, don't imagine that the tiles must be stuck on one by one. They can be bought attached to backing sheets, which makes it easy to apply blocks of them to large areas. Each sheet is glued on tile-side down, then the backing paper is peeled away when the adhesive is dry.

Suite: A curved or corner bath could be a good idea if your bathroom is an awkward shape. Although it occupies a similar floor area to a standard rectangular bath, it may allow space in areas where you need it – to allow room to open a door, for example. The deep sink has a traditional farmhouse style, and the simple plywood surround suits its utilitarian character.

BATHROOM TIP
Frosted or sandblasted glass ensures privacy. Give clear window or door panes a similar effect by applying glass etch spray, available from DIY stores. Mask off surrounding areas, then spray on several light coats

The look: With looks that could have come straight from a Manhattan apartment, this spacious room contrasts dark stone flooring with white walls and fittings to create a bold, modernist scheme.

Color: The strong contrast lends impact to an essentially simple scheme, where light and dark shades are balanced in equal quantities. The pale grey mosaic tiling around the bath almost blends with the white, offering a subtle variation in tone to soften its starkness. The blue wall lifts the look with a dash of cool color.

Suite: Earning their place in this strikingly modern setting, the fittings have no fussy details to disturb their rounded curves and clean lines, although the bow-fronted bath gets a subtle touch of interest from the strip of pale grey highlighting its curved edge. The contemporary toilet has a neat, compact design, while the sink's pedestal basin boasts a bowl of generous proportions. Chrome-plated taps complete the sleek up-to-date styling.

Floor: Real stone flooring has natural beauty and is extremely hardwearing, but is also expensive and can feel cold underfoot. If you want a cheaper alternative, vinyl designs include many good stone lookalikes that will leave more cash in your pocket and are cosier for bare feet.

Accessories: In a space where the flooring dominates, a tall narrow mirror above the basin acts as a visual device to draw the eye upwards, adding vertical interest to the room and impact to the blue wall. The blue is repeated behind the circular cutouts of the eye-catching contemporary artwork, which add a spot of bold but lively pattern to the plain scheme.

The look: This ultra-minimalist shower room uses all the tricks of form and design to create a beautifully spacious feel. Wall-mounted fixtures are the epitome of modern simplicity, while reflective materials and pale colors capitalize on light streaming through the large skylight windows.

Color: The white walls and ceiling maximize the feeling of space, and pale beige flooring keeps the look light while softening the overall effect. Continuing the tiling onto the walls of the shower area and the housing behind the fixtures creates a seamless look, enhancing the room's streamlined feel. The glass screen adds color while reflecting light, its cool aqua offset by the warm tan accents of the wooden window frames.

Suite: Wall-mounted fixtures are perfect for pared-down looks. Smart and simple, all their workings, such as cisterns and pipes, can be concealed behind a false wall. With the floor area left free, they also make cleaning easier.

Shower screen: Keeping things simple is the key to minimalist design, and a plain glass partition screens off the shower area as effectively as a fancy enclosure. Make sure you use safety glass that complies with the proper standards.

Windows: If you have a dingy bathroom that lies directly beneath a roof, skylight windows could help to lift the gloom. As they don't take up valuable wall space, you can make them as large as possible to flood the room with light. Another advantage is that they don't present privacy problems, so won't need dressing – unless, of course, you are overlooked by a high-rise building!

BATHROOM TIP
Towel racks linked to your heating system will not work in summer when it is turned off. If you want warm towels all year round, choose a rack connected to your hot water system, or one that is powered by an electric element

The look: Clean lines and clever storage have turned this small bathroom into a minimalist haven. Although it measures just 5.5 x 7ft, clearing out clutter and other furniture has allowed space for a generously sized bath and a chunky sink.

Color: All-white walls maximize the illusion of space and light in a tiny room, and using the same mosaic tiles on both walls and floor creates a seamless appearance. However, a white room needn't be a dull one. Liven things up with bold blocks of color – lime green covers the bath panelling, and the cabinet above the toilet is painted a rich magenta. Bright accessories, such as the bath mat, also add impact, while the silver shower curtain instils an air of contemporary glamour.

Suite: The fixtures have a streamlined look, thanks to an ingenious false wall, which conceals a spaghetti of pipework. The back-to-wall toilet has its tank attached to the real wall, but the false wall built over it leaves only the toilet bowl and handle visible. The components of the suite are all from different ranges: the compact toilet is teamed with a large, traditional-shaped basin and a roomy bath. The basin's trendy pillar faucet, designed by Philippe Starck, enhances the room's modern appeal.

Storage: Unobtrusive storage keeps clutter out of sight. The bathtub panels are hinged doors, which open to allow cleaning materials to be stashed behind them. Above the toilet, a broad but shallow cupboard with shelves inside provides space for toiletries.

BATHROOM TIP
If your bathroom is shared by children or elderly people, make sure it is safe and user-friendly for them. Helpful features include non-slip flooring or mats, easy-to-operate taps and rails beside the bath

The look: The powerful contrast between deep purple and bright yellow makes an enlivening color statement in this room, bringing a suite with classic styling bang up to date.

Color: This scheme shows how complementary colors – any two that lie directly opposite each other on the color wheel – can bring out the best in each other, forming a vibrant contrast rather than a nasty clash. When combining two strong colors, keep the deeper one for the lower part of the room. It 'grounds' the scheme, while the brighter shade keeps the atmosphere light and airy. Take the wall colors over shelves and skirtings for continuity.

Wood panelling: A bathroom without tiles knocks dollars off the budget. If you've moved the suite and damaged the walls, tongue-and-groove panelling is a quick cover-up; here it has been taken up to shoulder height and topped with a narrow shelf. Widely available from DIY stores, the boards are easy to fit and can be painted any color you like. Apply matte varnish after painting to protect them from damp.

Suite: Fixtures with a classic shape are ideal if you have modern tastes but live in an older house. It is complemented by traditional-style pillar taps and a dark wood toilet seat. Surrounding the bath with panelling that matches the walls allows the purple to make greater impact.

Accessories: A scheme of two bold colors needs touches of a third for balance, so accessories introduce flashes of sharp green. A beaded curtain is a lighthearted touch at the window. For extra privacy, hang a roller blind behind it or cover the window with etching spray, which gives the look of frosted glass.

The look: With the sleek simplicity of city style, this room combines a smart palette of greys and black with the fashionable glimmer of glass and silver. Compact contemporary fittings soften the look with their graceful curves.

Color: Unassuming greys give the room a relaxing feel; using different shades on the two walls adds interest to the overall effect. Black floor tiles drive home the smartness of the scheme, providing a bold contrast with the white skirtings and fittings. The sparkle of silver and glass accessories adds high-tech glamour.

Suite: The sculptural shapes of the fittings contrast with the straight lines of the walls, window and accessories, while their compact design enhances the room's modernist appeal. The close-coupled toilet has a slimline tank with neat push-button flush, and a pan that features smooth curves for easy cleaning. The semi-pedestal

design of the trendy wall-hung sink leaves no messy pipework on display, and its monoblock tap with single lever also has an unfussy modern look. A narrow strip of aqua-colored glass, fixed to the wall with three screws, makes a stylish splashback.

Lighting: As well as a background light source, bathrooms need efficient illumination near mirrors to provide good light for close-up tasks such as shaving or applying make-up. These vertical lamps echo the shape of the tall mirror and add glowing yellow accents to warm up the scheme.

Accessories: The geometric arrangement of mirror, glass shelves and lamps creates an attractive wall feature. The stylish laundry basket echoes the silvery sheen of the tap and freestanding chrome towel rail, while fresh flowers displayed in a black and silver vase add a further touch of luxury.

BATHROOM TIP
To save water, choose a tank that offers a choice of flushing modes. A dual control allows you to opt for a shorter flush when a longer burst of water is not necessary

The look: Blue and white is a popular color scheme for a bathroom, but original design ideas, such as the textured wall and extended bath surround, lift this one out of the ordinary.

Color: The contrast between blue and white creates a fresh, invigorating feel. A textured, rough-plaster effect softens the austerity of the white walls, while the woodgrain of the bath surround and the woodstain effect of the flooring add a natural dimension to the deep blues. The colorful mosaic tiles, in a medley of blues and aquas, add pattern and pace to the scheme.

Bath: Boxing in the bath with a surround that continues beyond its end not only adds a stylish feature to the room but also creates a handy ledge that can be used for sitting on after a bath and as a display area for toiletries or plants. The surround is constructed from timber, and the sides are painted with a blue woodstain. Mosaic tiles create a fashionable, wipe-clean surface for the top.

Walls: The rough wall finish is created by mixing powdered tile adhesive into a thick paste and applying it with spreaders. To get a patterned effect, press a rubber doormat or other textured surface into the paste before it dries to imprint the design. Paint in the color of your choice, then add a coat of clear acrylic varnish for a damp-resistant finish.

Floor: The floor is covered in trendy blue laminate planks, with strips of darker blue inserted at an angle to add interest. Their woodstain effect matches the finish on the side of the bath surround, and a wooden duckboard makes a coordinating bath mat.

The look: Clean up with white walls, flooring and fittings for a sparkling modern scheme. Bands of mint and aqua tiles add subtle color while keeping the look as refreshing as a toothpaste ad.

Color: There's nothing like white for clearing out the cobwebs and replacing them with a spotless environment. Using white throughout will defeat dinginess in a small room and make a large space dazzlingly bright. Inject a dash of color to lift its clinical feel though – soft shades of mint and aqua are complemented by deeper turquoise accents in the towels and glass vase.

Suite: Compact fixtures with smooth curves are perfectly compatible with the pristine contemporary decor. Wall-mounted pieces, such as the sink, have an especially neat look, and allow for easy cleaning of the floor area below. Gleaming chrome adds high-tech shine and coordinates all the details in the room, from the taps and toothbrush holder to the trim surrounding the glass door of the shower stall.

Tiles: Using tiles to cover both the walls and floor makes for an easy-clean bathroom. They can look monotonous, but the bands of colored tiles break up the high walls, their subtle sponged effect providing additional interest. Using brick-shaped tiles on the floor also varies the effect a little.

Window: A sheer roller blind in a pale aqua provides both privacy and color without blocking out light. Roller blinds are available in a range of sizes, or you can make one by using your own fabric and buying the fittings separately. These are sold in kits, and you can cut the roller to fit the width of your window.

BATHROOM TIP
For truly clean looks, keep your fixtures free of limescale. To remove it, apply a mixture of equal parts of hot vinegar and salt using a toothbrush, and leave until it can be scrubbed off

CONTEMPORARY

The look: An up-to-the-minute color scheme, concealed storage, and fixtures that combine designer looks with the latest technology mean this room scores highly on both form and function.

Color: Aqua walls and white tiles make a refreshing combination, and sleek metallic fittings and accessories enhance its cool, modern appeal. The tan bathtub panelling and sink add a hint of warmth, while the rubber flooring grounds the scheme with a deeper shade of blue.

Suite: A double-ended bathtub with smart central spigot and plug means no more debates about who sits at the tap end! This bath also has thermostatic settings that allow water to be set at a specific temperature. The round sink unit is another state-of-the-art design that fits neatly into a corner. Its semi-concealed shelving keeps toiletries tidily hidden but close at hand.

Storage: Flat MDF doors make an unobtrusive frontage for cupboards set into the space above the sink. Painted in a mix of colors, they are also drilled with holes so lights fitted inside can shine through. The door directly over the sink doubles as a surface for a mirror. More cupboard space is included in the triangular structure beside the bath.

Towel rack: A heated rack keeps towels toasty. If you want it to heat the room too, choose one that includes a radiator function as others won't provide enough warmth. It can be mounted high on the wall to save space – just make sure everyone can reach the towels.

BATHROOM TIP
Be aware of safety when planning your lighting. Electricity plus water equals danger, so make sure any fittings you buy are suitable for bathrooms. Lights should be turned on using a pull cord or a switch outside the room

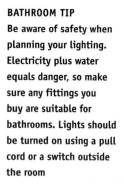

The look: Get the elements of urban chic with cool colors, innovative designs and reflective materials, such as glass and chrome, all brought together in a minimalist scheme.

Color: Refreshing colors and pale woods ensure a bright, modern feel. Light from the overhead window glances off white walls and smooth wood flooring, while aqua-colored tiling gives the shower enclosure a more inviting atmosphere. The walls are covered mostly in glass mosaics, but borders of standard-sized turquoise tiles help to link the white and aqua areas. Scarlet towels bring the scheme to life with splashes of hot color.

Shower: If you don't want to fit a bath, then make the most of your shower by surrounding it with a spacious walk-in enclosure. This gives you plenty of room to move around, and means that two people can share a shower comfortably. Clear glass walls help to maintain the illusion of space, and even increase it by reflecting light. A DIY alternative would be to build a glass brick stall.

Basin: Many small sinks feature state-of-the-art shapes, colors and materials. Providing a stylish focal point at the far end of the room, this simple curved bowl made from aqua-colored glass sits in a freestanding unit that provides counter space on either side. Taps are mounted on the wall above.

Accessories: The large round mirror echoes the curves of the sink, boosting its decorative effect. In the corner below, a discreet chrome rack keeps toiletries under control, saving them from cluttering the countertop.

The look: Crisp and clean, this scheme combines polished metal and pristine white for the purest take on bathroom style. Pale blue walls complement the cool, clinical mood, while a dose of bright red helps to energize the look.

Color: Fittings and furniture with white or metallic finishes ensure a modern, high-tech feel, but medical chic needs a dash of color to make it livable. A fresh mid-tone shade of blue is sufficiently intense to give the room a more intimate feel, but also looks cool and clean. Painting the upper part of the walls in a lighter shade maintains the airy atmosphere. The towels bring the blues to life with warmer colors and stimulating stripes, while accents of black in the mosaic tiles and mirror frame add depth to the pale scheme.

Suite and furniture: You don't have to buy a matching suite – combine pieces from different collections to suit your needs. If you can manage without a full-size sink, a tiny one like this will fit easily into the smallest bathroom. Use the space you save to slide in a generous storage cabinet, which includes closed cupboards to help you keep the room clutter-free. Metal surfaces not only suit this look but also earn their keep in small spaces by bouncing light around. The bath is boxed in with plywood covered with panels of stainless steel.

Accessories: Chrome accessories add further metallic shine, the tall ladder making a striking towel rail. The white shower curtain is made from kite fabric, which is cheap to buy.

BATHROOM TIP
If bath oils leave greasy marks on metal surfaces, wipe them away using methylated spirit

The look: Form follows function in this cutting-edge bathroom. The sink and toilet are by celebrated designer Philippe Starck, and a superbly simple Italian bath takes center stage.

Color: A blend of pale blues and greys creates a sophisticated backdrop for state-of-the-art fittings, the soft smoky shade on the walls harmonizing with the iridescent greeny-grey of the floor tiles. Mirror-like metallics enhance the air of high-tech chic, while wood surfaces introduce a touch of warmth to make the cool scheme feel more friendly. Towels add subtle accent colors of muted jade, lilac and cream.

Suite: Shape is an important element of style, especially where bathroom suites are concerned. With their combination of straight lines and flowing modern curves, these fittings epitomize 21st-century cool. The close-coupled floorstanding toilet has a wonderfully slimline tank, and the bowl shares the distinctive conical shaping of the bidet and freestanding sink. Placing the generously sized bathtub in the center of the room, and at an angle, shows off its shape to advantage and turns it into a focal point.

Storage: A gleaming chrome cabinet on wheels provides high-style storage, and can be moved wherever it's needed. The small wooden drawer unit attached to the mirror base is handy for stashing small items, such as cosmetics, while a simple wall-mounted shelf keeps everyday essentials within reach.

Floor: Laminate sheet flooring that resembles glass mosaic squares is perfect for a chic, contemporary scheme. Although rather pricey as laminates go, it's a worthwhile investment, combining the iridescent shimmer and reflective qualities of real glass with a practical, hardwearing surface.

The look: Deep turquoise and watery aquas create a feeling of well-being and harmony. Team them with a mix of traditional fittings and modern furniture for an intensely relaxing bathroom.

Color: A combination of closely toning shades creates a look that has visual interest yet, with no strong contrasts to jar the eye, exudes a wonderfully calming mood. This room uses blocks of soft blue and aqua on the walls, and juxtaposes floor tiles of similar harmonious shades. White fixtures and woodwork, plus the punchier turquoise of the bathtub and splashback, give the look a more upbeat feel.

Suite: If you want a bathroom that encourages you to pamper yourself, generously proportioned traditional fixtures will add an air of luxury to the most modern setting. A freestanding roll-top bath with elaborate claw feet makes an inviting centerpiece, and blends in perfectly when painted in the room's colors. The large sink also has a commanding presence, with angular moldings and classic-style taps. A neat splashback of toughened glass offsets its traditional looks.

Furniture: The shelf unit and director's chair reassert the modern feel created by the cool blues. The sleek chrome shelving adds a high-tech glimmer, and provides display space for colorful accessories. The wooden chair introduces a more casual note, while enhancing the air of comfort.

Floor: Choosing flooring in a similar color to the walls ensures a relaxing atmosphere, and if you opt for ceramic tiles you're sure to find shades to match. There is an enormous range available, and they make a relatively inexpensive floorcovering. Try using colors to create interesting effects – here two tones arranged in barely perceptible stripes create a subtle watery look.

The look: Unfussy design works best in small spaces, but they needn't miss out on character. This shower stall gives contemporary simplicity a Victorian twist. Reproduction taps and a bathhouse-style floor evoke the 19th-century feel, while glass shelving and 'dressing-room' lighting bring the look right up to date.

Color: A combination of black, white and cream is a smart but simple choice for this tiny room. The cream-colored walls have a space-enhancing effect but give a softer, more traditional look than pure white. Using two different kinds of tiles adds interest – those on the lower wall have a more textured, glazed finish than the flat, matte ones above – and separating them with a line of dark blue pencil tiles gives the impression of a Victorian dado rail. Against this restrained backdrop, the checkerboard flooring makes a strong style statement, its boldly contrasting black and white tiles adding impact as well as character to the room.

Suite: The clean, contemporary lines of the basin and loo keep the overall look simple, their smooth curves contrasting with the geometric checks of the flooring. However, the old-fashioned pillar taps enhance the Victorian feel, showing how important details can be in adding style to a room.

Shower: If you opt for a shower instead of a bath, choose a large enclosure to give it a more luxurious feel. A glass door will prevent it from making your room feel cramped – choose one that opens inwards to save space.

Accessories: A sleek chrome bin and a slim glass shelf balance the Victorian elements with contemporary chic. In this small space, toiletries are kept to a minimum to avoid clutter.

The look: Inspired by pared-down oriental style, this room achieves its minimalism with modern space-saving fittings, their pipework cleverly concealed behind a false wall underneath the window. A plain and simple color scheme enhances the clean lines.

Color: Painting the false wall white allows the suite to blend in with the background and, aided by the natural light that finds its way through the large window, gives the room a bright, airy feel. The aqua-colored glass partition and the grey, industrial-style floor tiles underline the scheme's modernism by adding smart contemporary color and texture, while the pale ash panelling softens the look slightly with subtle wood tones.

Suite: An up-to-the-minute suite with smooth curves will give the smallest bathroom a sleek look. Try to fit the bathtub, sink and toilet in a line to give you as much clear floor space as possible. The false wall that encases the tank and the pipework of the semi-recessed sink gives the room an especially streamlined appearance. It also creates a deep multipurpose ledge, which serves as storage and display area, sink countertop and windowsill.

Wood panelling: Tongue-and-groove panelling is commonly found in country-style bathrooms, but these pale ash boards, hung horizontally, give a sleek modern look. Protect them from water by applying several layers of matte polyurethane varnish.

Accessories: With no space for a mirror near the sink, a tall chrome totem topped by a small shaving mirror provides a neat solution. With a shelf for toiletries, plus a rack for clothes or towels, it comprises several accessories in one and is easy to move around. A potted orchid reflects the room's oriental inspiration.

BATHROOM TIP
Planning is the most important aspect of fitting out a bathroom. To optimize your space, take advantage of the expert advice and computer-aided design packages offered by some bathroom companies

The look: A tiny bathroom may present you with limited layout options, but clever design ideas can make it feel less cramped. Simple decor, large mirrors and unobtrusive glass shelving help to maximize the space in this narrow room.

Color: In a very small room, restrict your main palette to just two plain shades – you can always add tiny amounts of accent color to liven up the look. White is an obvious choice if you want to increase the feeling of space; this room softens the effect by teaming it with a calming shade of aqua. Using the two shades as plain blocks of color keeps the look simple – the white is used for the tiles and upper walls, while the green covers all the wood-panelled surfaces.

Suite: The toilet slides neatly into the alcove at the end of the room, but the standard-width bath leaves only a very narrow area alongside. A tapered bath may be a better option in a cramped room; while allowing plenty of space at the tap end, where you stand to use the shower attachment, it narrows towards the other to increase floor space.

Shelves: As well as having clean, contemporary appeal, glass shelves give a more open look than those made from solid materials. These are supported by discreet white brackets that blend in with the wall.

Mirror: Every bathroom needs at least one mirror, so make full use of their space-enhancing properties. Large mirrors visually expand a small room by reflecting space and light, and placing one on a long wall in a narrow room like this can make it feel twice as wide.

The look: Every bathroom needs storage, and with clever planning you can fit plenty into even the smallest space. This room uses built-in units to provide cube storage and cupboard space as well as to enclose the concealed parts of the toilet, bidet and sink.

Color: A mix of smart but relaxing neutrals gives the room its sophisticated contemporary character. The dark grey panelling and black countertop create an air of urban chic and highlight the elegant lines of the white suite. The warmer beige of the wall cupboards has a more easy-going feel, while the flecked carpet combines both key colors to add a hint of cosy texture.

Suite: The smooth oval curves of the suite are complemented by chrome taps with stylish conical tops, and the toilet completes the look of modern simplicity with a neat push-button flush. A semi-inset sink and back-to-wall toilet can be built into fitted units, which ensure clean lines by hiding away the tank and pipework. Some bathroom companies supply units and bath panels designed to accompany their suites; the ones in this room come primed and ready to paint in your choice of color.

Storage: Fitting a unit around a sink makes good use of the area below; this one has cupboard doors that allow access to storage space inside. On the wall above, a grid of wooden cubes with flat painted doors provides further unobtrusive storage.

Floor: Although it makes a warm and comfortable floorcovering, carpet may not stand up well to steam and splashes. Avoid deep-pile designs, fit an underlay to ensure good wear and keep a bath mat handy to protect the surface.

The look: Rehanging the door made way for a more user-friendly layout in this small room. Decorating throughout in similar shades enhances the new-found sense of space, while simple modern storage cubes turn clutter into art.

Layout: The door previously opened to the right, which severely restricted the layout options. Rehanging the door allows for a neater layout, with the bathtub, sink and toilet in a line along one wall. Hanging a door so that it opens outwards, rather than into the bathroom, would save even more space.

Color: Light rosy shades take the chill off a room without having the cramping effect of deeper pinks. To retain a sense of space, stick to a palette of similar shades, rather than heavy contrasts which will appear to cut the room into sections. The dusky wall color is repeated in the mottled splashback tiles, and tones harmoniously with the neutral stone flooring. Further natural color and texture is added by the woven window blind and storage boxes.

Suite: Compact fixtures with clean lines fit easily into the space available. The toilet has a slim, modern tank, which takes up little horizontal wall space, leaving plenty of room for the sink. A glass shower screen allows an unobstructed view across the room.

Storage: Simple MDF cubes require little wall space but provide useful storage and display areas. To make them, cut pieces of 1cm-thick MDF for each side and sand the edges lightly. Drill small pilot holes in each side and screw the boxes together. Paint with an eggshell finish, then hang from mirror plates.

BATHROOM TIP
Using large-scale furnishings in a small room can trick the eye. Big tiles appear to enlarge a floor area, while hanging a sizeable picture on the wall may also create a surprisingly spacious feel

The look: With a sophisticated shower unit and designer fittings, this room is the height of high-tech. It also shows how effectively white walls and mirrored and glass surfaces can boost the impression of space and light.

Color: The bright blue flooring, with its wacky wave design, brings color and a touch of fun to the pristine white environment. The clean, clinical quality of the decor suits the room's high-tech style, but white has also been chosen because it has the ability to make a space feel brighter and airier than any other color.

Suite: Designed by Philippe Starck, the distinctive modern shapes of the toilet and sink add to the room's space-age feel. The more conventional bath is neatly boxed in beside the shower unit with a simple white panel. Mirrored walls create a water-proof splashback which, by reflecting the entire room, makes it feel considerably more spacious than it actually is.

Shower: The shower stall is another miracle of reflection, with mirrors covering its inside walls and a clear glass door that lets light flow freely. Stall doors should be made from toughened safety glass.

Floor: The flooring is Marmoleum, a linoleum-style covering made from natural raw materials such as linseed oil, chalk and pine resin. It is available in many colors and designs, but this wavy pattern has been created by cutting out dark blue and white shapes and inserting them mosaic-style into the bright blue background. The flooring curves up the walls to avoid the danger of damp.

BATHROOM TIP
If you want a shower that's separate from your bath but can't fit in both, consider placing a freestanding unit elsewhere. A self-contained shower stall can slide into an understairs cupboard or a corner of a bedroom, as long as there is adequate ventilation

The look: How do you squeeze standard-sized fixtures and plenty of storage into a room of just 4 x 6.5ft and still achieve a refreshingly spacious feel? Careful planning, clever shopping and a light-friendly color scheme can make that dream a reality.

Color: Fuss-free white walls and matching fixtures can work like magic in a small room, creating a bright, contemporary scheme that really opens up the space. However, don't get too hung up on the plain and simple idea – a dash of decoration saves a tiny bathroom from that broom-cupboard feeling. Mosaic-effect wall tiles, with an elegant leafy border, lift the look by adding pattern, texture and interest. The timber countertop also relieves the iciness of the white with its natural warmth.

Suite: Shop around for fittings that suit your needs. This bath tapers slightly at the other end, creating more floor space where it's needed, yet is still big enough for an adult to stretch out in. As the bath falls short of the room's length, a timber box has been created to fill the gap, and this extends to forma countertop for the sink. A semi-recessed sink offers the comfort of a full-sized basin but can be set into a narrower-than-standard unit to give a feeling of space. Its slick looks are complemented by a modern designer-style tap with easy-to-operate lever control.

Storage: Boxing in the area below the sink creates closed cupboard space for towels and cleaning materials, while the open shelf unit above keeps toiletries more conveniently within reach. Wicker pots add natural character.

SPACE-SAVING

The look: With the trend for having more bathrooms within a house, it's tempting to try and squeeze an extra one into a corner of a converted loft. This scheme distracts attention from the room's small proportions by adding character with color. A skylight window helps to brighten the atmosphere.

Color: A deep shade of lilac has a stimulating effect in such a small space, and is used on both the walls and ceiling for maximum impact. However, it does not seem too overpowering: applying it as a colorwash helps to soften its strength, and it is balanced with plenty of fresh white. The wide white horizontal stripes break up the expanse of lilac and heighten the vibrant contrast between the two colors. Towels enliven the white suite with accents of hot pink, while metal accessories and wooden details add hints of natural color and texture.

Suite: Although the wide sink and tank seem rather a tight fit in this small space, the traditional moldings and generous proportions of the suite have a certain air of luxury about them that adds to the style of the room. There's nothing to stop you from placing fittings in close proximity side by side as long as you allow enough sitting or standing space in front for them to serve their purpose.

Window: Loft rooms have a reputation for being dingy, so if you plan to convert yours, it's worth getting skylight windows fitted in the sloping roof. Unless your room is overlooked from above they won't need dressing, although you can buy blinds specially designed for them.

BATHROOM TIP
Before planning a loft conversion, ask your local authority whether you need planning permission. If it's to include a bathroom, seek the advice of an experienced plumber before any work begins

The look: However small your bathroom, don't let size cramp your style. Distinctive furnishings, such as a glass sink and round mosaic tiles, will outshine its tiny dimensions. The boy/girl bath mat and wordy shower curtain add graphic detail to this slick modern scheme.

Color: Aqua blue is a popular choice for contemporary bathrooms. Cool but welcoming, this mid-tone shade creates a bold impact which is balanced by the lighter colors of the off-white mosaic tiles and pale blue glass-effect laminate flooring.

Suite: The room is just wide enough to fit a standard-sized 5.5ft bath along one side. A wall-mounted sink frees up floor space; although relatively pricey, this glass bowl in azure blue makes a stylish focal point. A close-coupled toilet also saves space. Its sleek shape goes perfectly with the slightly industrial look of the room, as do the wall-mounted spout and crosshead tap controls.

Splashback: Round mosaic tiles are more expensive than standard square ones, but in a tiny space they give priceless individuality. Using colored grout – these white tiles are finished with grey – also gives an original look.

Storage: Clever chrome shelves above the toilet utilize space that is normally wasted. It has rungs for towels, and shelves of varying depths for toiletries, plus a cupboard with frosted glass doors for items best kept hidden. Another practical idea is a freestanding ladder on wheels which can be placed over the radiator to dry towels.

BATHROOM TIP
To form a clean edge when grouting mosaic tiles, place a piece of cardstock or board the same thickness as the tiles along the finished edge. Grout up to and over the card, then carefully remove it

BATHROOM TIP

Adding small dividing walls not only adds interest to a room but can also make it easier to plan a space-saving layout. If existing wall area is limited, a partition beside a bath, for instance, can create a surface to set a sink against

The look: Deep color can work wonders in small spaces, adding drama, warmth and character. In this oriental-style room, boxing in the suite ensures clean lines, allowing pale wood, buff mosaic and rose pink to create a welcoming mix.

Color: Although light, cool colors give the illusion of space, deep, warm shades will make your room feel cosier. To enhance the space you have, choose plain shades rather than patterned, and balance a deep color with pale wood or lighter tiles. Bronze mosaics tone closely with birch panelling to give the lower half of this room a uniform look. Although less intense than the pink, they are rich enough to complement its warmth, bringing a glow to the whole room. Ceramic floor tiles in a pale neutral provide a calmer base.

Suite: Compact fixtures with simple modern taps suit this minimalist look, but it's the structures around them that give the room its character. Combining natural warmth with streamlined styling, birch laminate panels fixed onto battens are used to box in both the bath and sink, a door below the sink giving access to useful storage capacity inside. Adding a small partition between the sink and bath helps to break up the space, and could even be fully tiled to form a practical shower screen. Continuing the mosaic tiling onto the tops of the surrounds gives a neat, water-resistant finish.

Accessories: Bamboo accessories reinforce the room's oriental feel. To make bamboo cupboard handles, screw two blocks of plywood to the door, then glue short lengths of bamboo to these using heavy-duty adhesive. Other accessories such as stone pots, woven baskets and a simple flower arrangement are also in character.

The look: A small space doesn't mean you can't think big. This room manages to fit in a large bath and sink as well as carrying off some bold floor and wall tiles. A calming blend of aqua greens brings them all into harmony.

Color: The mix of greens and blues creates a refreshing but relaxing atmosphere in this small, dark bathroom. The pale aqua green walls keep the mood airy, while the bath is painted a deeper shade for contrast. Dark blue floor tiles smarten up the look, and the medley of watery green wall tiles also packs a punch.

Suite: If you want to fit a large bath into a small space, opt for depth over length. A roll-top bath combines character with a generous bathing area, and can be painted to match your scheme. Don't let size dictate the agenda when it comes to other fixtures; a tiny modern sink may save space, but this sturdy traditional design makes a much better partner for the period-style bath.

Splashback: Less is often more when it comes to wall tiles. In a cramped space, a large expanse of colorful tiling might look overpowering, whereas a small splashback above a sink adds just enough impact. Using fewer tiles also means you can afford to indulge in pricey but beautiful handmade designs.

Floor: The same principle applies to flooring: with only a small area to cover, you might find the pennies to splash out on a style-statement floorcovering. Real stone tiles are expensive to buy, and should be professionally fitted, but these silvery blue slate slabs fit in perfectly with the color scheme.

The look: Clever use of color and a suite designed for small spaces help to broaden the horizons of this narrow bathroom, which measures just 4ft wide. Boxed-in pipework and a neat storage cabinet also contribute to its clean, contemporary look.

Color: Three shades of green give the room a bright but soothing atmosphere, and form a subtle contrast with the white suite and mosaic tiles. Painting the shades in broad bands around the walls makes the room feel wider, a useful decorating trick if you want to expand a narrow space.

Suite: Tiny bathrooms are a common breed, so manufacturers are responding to the demand for scaled-down fittings. This tiny suite includes a bathtub only 46in long, just the right size to fit across the width of the room. The toilet and sink, also smaller than most other models, have been fitted side by side to allow a clear run of floor space through from the door to the bath.

Wood panelling: Exposed pipework looks bad enough in a large bathroom, but in an area of this size it's a real eyesore. Boxing in the pipes with tongue-and-groove boards not only keeps them out of sight but also creates an extra shelf. The bath is boxed in too, and painting all the panelling to match the adjacent band of wall color gives the lower part of the room a clean, seamless appearance.

Storage: Make efficient use of space with multifunctional items, such as cabinet doors that double as mirrors. This wall-mounted cupboard swallows up toiletries and cosmetics, leaving basin and bath surrounds clear and preventing clutter from killing the sensation of space.

The look: Country-style accessories and dashes of ginger add spice to this cream bathroom. The towel rack and minimal window dressing also warm things up by boosting heat and light levels.

Color: Decorating with cream not only makes a small space feel bright and airy but also creates a go-with-anything backdrop. If you like to change your decor frequently, it's simpler to renew accessories rather than repaint walls or tiles. Window dressings, towels and soaps all offer easy ways of introducing character-forming color. Here a Roman blind in crisp ginger and white ticking adds spicy warmth to the window area, while a burnt orange bath towel makes a bolder statement. Other accessories enhance the country feel with natural color.

Bath: Boxing in a bath with wood panelling gives a neat look and allows you to paint the surround to match your walls. If you have the space, including a ledge around the top creates an attractive display area for pretty accessories.

Towel rack: The heated towel rack beside the bath means that warm, dry towels are never far away. If you want a rack that will heat your room as well, choose a model designed to double as a radiator. Towel racks come in many sizes – a tall one provides ample hanging space.

Accessories: A country look relies on natural materials and textures as well as colors. A bamboo bath rack makes a perfect finishing touch, and the woven laundry basket and stone candleholder also reinforce the look.

The look: Look to foreign lands for colorful country style. This bathroom's maritime scheme was inspired by the vibrant blues and greens of the seas around Greece. Panelled walls and painted wooden furniture show them off beautifully.

Color: Different tones of blue mix comfortably together, and greens blend well with them to create a harmonious scheme. A spectrum of sea shades gives this room its welcoming, summery feel – from deepest indigo on the bath to brighter blue and jade on wood panelling and furniture, through to soft aqua on the upper walls. Using a lighter shade for the top half of the room helps to freshen the atmosphere.

Wall panelling: Wood panelling creates a warmer, more natural feel than tiled walls, and is widely used in country-style rooms. As tongue-and-groove boards can be painted in any color, they make a versatile wallcovering that can be decorated to suit a variety of different moods. This dado-height panelling is edged with a wide wooden beading that provides a useful display area for seashore accessories such as shells and starfish.

Suite: A traditional roll-top bath is ideal for creating that old-fashioned, unfitted feel and, like the wall panelling, can be painted to boost the room's color power. A wood-effect seat adds rustic style to the loo.

Furniture: Keep the color show going by painting old wooden furniture. Sand down the wood, or use a multi-surface primer if it's already painted or varnished, then apply gloss or satin-finish color. Add a coat of varnish as protection against splashes of water. The simple green chest has been further revamped by adding a wavy plinth cut from MDF, plus new wooden drawer knobs.

The look: A complete white-wash will open up a small bathroom, making it feel amazingly bright and spacious. To prevent it feeling cold, subtle color accents and characterful accessories have been added.

Color: Painting both walls and ceiling in white will certainly appear to expand space. If this idea appeals, add interest with textured surfaces – wood panelling looks less clinical than white tiles, and the woven chair has natural texture. Color accents lift the look, but this scheme retains its understated calm by sticking to neutral shades. The greys of the patterned flooring are echoed by the silvery glimmer of the taps and metallic items. Wooden accessories add warmer splashes of color.

Suite: The traditional design of the suite and taps also helps to soften the look, creating a more laid-back feel than sleek modern fittings. Boxing in the bathtub with panelling that matches the walls creates a streamlined effect.

Chair: The classic Lloyd Loom chair adds an air of old-fashioned comfort. If you want to change the color of a woven chair, use spray paint. Work in a well-ventilated room and cover surrounding surfaces, then apply several light coats.

Accessories: Choose accessories that add character as well as color. For a lived-in feel, include items that have seen better days, such as the old mirror and distressed medicine cabinet. The folding stool adds a further casual touch, in contrast with the smarter metal accessories.

The look: Wooden floorboards and wall panelling painted in cool cream give this bathroom an airy modern-country feel, while louvred shutters and carved wood add touches of colonial style.

Color: Light colors create a sense of space, and cream gives a clean and simple look that's easy to live with. The wood-panelled walls and bath surround are painted with eggshell to match the sanded floorboards, giving the small room a spacious, streamlined feel. A closely toning shade on the walls continues the seamless look, while a sparkling white suite crisps up the cream. Accents of rich terracotta and dark brown add hints of exotic style to warm up the cool surroundings.

Suite: The suite teams classic Victorian styling with lean contours, which save space in a relatively small room. Panelling the bath with tongue-and-groove boards and opting for a mahogany-effect toilet seat gives

the fixtures a softer, country-style appearance.

Furniture: A dark wood Moroccan cupboard and a pine-framed mirror, both with decorative carving, add character to the room. The wall-mounted cabinet with glass-panelled doors provides tidy storage for toiletries while keeping its contents on view. It is painted to match the scheme, with cream on the outside and terracotta inside.

Window: Colonial-style shutters complement the ethnic appeal of the Moroccan cupboard. Their adjustable louvred panels allow full control over light levels.

The look: Make that holiday mood last all year round with a bathroom that brings the seaside closer to home. A candy-striped deck chair and a sky-blue tub, cast adrift on a sea of ocean-blue flooring, are constant reminders of lazy days on the beach.

Color: Floorboards painted in deep blue and finished with clear varnish have the color and shimmering quality of calm seas, and unfitted furniture shows them off to advantage. They are complemented by the paler blue used to highlight the bath, while the soft lilac on the lower walls enhances the relaxing feel of the scheme. White provides a crisp contrast, bringing a breath of fresh air to the room, and the pretty pink stripes of the deck chair also help to lighten the mood.

Bath: A large, old-fashioned bath is the central feature of this laid-back look. What's more, its shape is reminiscent of the hull of a boat. The burnished gold finish on its feet introduces a luxurious touch of glamour.

Chair: Who says deck chairs are only for outdoors? Imaginative use of furniture is an easy way of adding character to a bathroom, and this chair gives an instant seaside feel. If you want to replace the sling of a deck chair to match your scheme, choose a tough canvas or other strong cotton fabric.

Accessories: The large wall map above the bath hints romantically at distant shores, while its aqua background introduces a further dose of sea-inspired color.

BATHROOM TIP
Cast-iron bathtubs are not only extremely durable but also retain heat better than acrylic fixtures, which means your bath water stays hotter for longer

The look: Pretty florals and delicate pastels set the tone for a comfortable country-cottage bathroom steeped in tradition. Slip in modern materials such as Lucite and laminate to edge the look into the 21st century.

Color: Pastels such as muted pinks, mint green and lilacs form the color palette for this feminine look, but its most important ingredient is flowers. Look for traditional floral patterns, especially on wallpaper. If you want to combine a number of different prints, give your scheme a unified look by making sure they all contain one common color, such as pink. To prevent the scheme becoming overfussy, offset the floral walls and fabric with plenty of plain color in painted or tiled surfaces.

Suite: No hard lines are allowed for this look, so choose a suite with curvy contours. A rounded modern sink looks perfectly at home in this nostalgic setting when teamed with traditional taps in gleaming chrome. The semi-countertop design is built into a wooden unit painted in pale green to match the chair and bath surround. Wood-effect laminate gives the top a waterproof covering, while a Lucite splashback protects the wallpaper.

Floor: Ceramic tiles provide hard-wearing, low-maintenance flooring and give a clean, contemporary look. To complement the pastel palette, choose a soft, livable neutral that looks relaxingly natural rather than rustic.

Accessories: Shower caps and laundry bags offer the opportunity to introduce further floral romance, while wicker baskets and touches of wood give country authenticity. Add comfort with a painted wooden chair with rush seat, plus fluffy towels in natural or pretty colors. Scented toiletries with old-fashioned packaging complete the look.

BATHROOM TIP
Displaying well-chosen toiletries is an easy way of adding character or color to your room. Many brands have smart or decorative packaging, while bath oils come in a range of delicious colors, from modern brights to country-style neutrals

The look: Inspired by chic 1930s looks, this simple but sophisticated scheme combines a smart Art Deco-style suite with a more decorative Arts and Crafts feel created by wood-panelled walls and floral details.

Color: Light blue makes a refreshing choice for this small bathroom, filling it with uplifting color without compromising its feeling of space. Pale grey flooring harmonizes with the cool blue to give the overall look a calming effect, while the white suite provides a crisp contrast.

Walls: Panelling the walls up to picture-rail height makes the small but high-ceilinged room look more in proportion by breaking up the vertical space. This effect has been emphasized by painting the wall above the panelling a few tones lighter and topping it with a plate rack detail that provides a display space for decorative accessories. The panelling comprises waterproof MDF boards made to look like tongue and groove.

Suite: A toilet with angular lines inspired by Art Deco design adds shape and style. The chunky bath also makes its presence felt, its outsize dimensions defying the limited space within the room to instil an air of luxury. Panelling it to match the walls makes it look less imposing by helping it to blend in with the background.

Accessories: The row of pretty floral pictures on the plate rack creates an eye-catching display and picks up on the Arts and Crafts influence. They are made from swatches of fabric slipped into white-painted wooden frames. A floral-print laundry bag echoes their country charm, while other accessories, such as the chrome laundry bin and glass-fronted medicine cabinet, have a sleeker, contemporary feel.

The look: The earthy colors and textures of old Provençal buildings inspired this casual country look, where a curvy modern suite blends comfortably with distressed furniture and rustic, stone-like effects on walls and floor.

Color: Gentle colors of nature – sage green, warm terracotta and pale neutrals – give the room its relaxing atmosphere. However, it's the textural effects that create the timeworn charm of a traditional French farmhouse. Softly colorwashed walls have the look of old sandstone, while the ceramic floor tiles are designed to resemble real terracotta. Painting the vanity unit and shutters with a distressed finish gives a deliberately shabby look.

Paint effects: For a colorwash like this, select two shades of sand-colored emulsion, one light, the other several shades darker. Apply the paler color and leave to dry. Dilute the other with water until it is the strength you want, then apply using a wide brush and crisscross strokes. To distress wooden furniture, paint with a pale neutral shade, then rub candlewax on areas that might suffer wear, such as panel edges. Apply green paint, then rub back the waxed parts with steel wool to expose patches of base coat.

Suite: Sleek contemporary fixtures and taps add an air of modern comfort to this traditional setting, their rounded curves enhancing the room's relaxed feel. Building the sink into a distressed vanity unit heightens the contrast between old and new.

Accessories: Glazed terracotta pots, slipware bowls and chunky natural-colored soaps help to create the Provençal feel. More unusual details, such as the candelabra, add character. If they're in season, fresh sunflowers arranged in a toning pitcher add the perfect finishing touch.

The look: Glowing yellow and other primary hues brighten up this tiny bathroom with the feelgood shades and vivid color contrasts of the Caribbean. Lightly whitewashed tongue-and-groove panelling recreates the sun-bleached look of a tropical beach-house.

Color: The brilliant yellow on the walls ensures that the sun never stops shining, a guaranteed cure for a dingy bathroom. In a small room, balancing this strong shade with plenty of fresh white helps to maintain the feeling of space. The large picture that covers most of one wall softens the strength of the yellow but livens up the look with additional vibrant color, its big abstract blocks lending the room a strikingly modern feel. Dark blue bath towels also add impact by creating a strong contrast with the yellow.

Wood panelling: The tongue-and-groove panelling on the side of the bathtub and the lower part of the walls offsets the powerful colors and abstract art to give the room a more relaxed, rural atmosphere. The white paint finish preserves the natural appeal of the wood by allowing the grain and knotting to show through, suggesting a sun-bleached appearance. To get this effect, simply dilute white emulsion with water – add a little at a time and experiment on a scrap board until you achieve the strength you want. When the painted panelling is dry, protect it from damp by applying a few coats of clear matte varnish.

Accessories: A crude storage box, made from an old wooden packing crate mounted on the wall, enhances the room's driftwood appeal, while the big seashell on top directly links its inspiration to tropical shores.

The look: If traditional country style is too fussy for your taste but you want a bathroom with plenty of interest, try this relaxing look that combines pale, modern colors and a contemporary suite with natural textures and accessories.

Color: The refreshing aqua on the walls is offset by the soft, natural color of the splashback tiles, creating a light but inviting atmosphere. Paler color schemes in bathrooms can tend to look rather stark and cold, especially with white woodwork, but this is counteracted by textural touches, such as the green slate-effect flooring and linen blind. Dark wood isn't always the first choice for bathroom accessories but the mahogany-colored cabinet helps to add definition to the overall look.

Suite: With a versatile contemporary design that would suit a range of different settings, the fixtures combine clean styling with gentle curves, and the modern taps have simple rounded knobs in white. The hand-held shower attachment can be fixed into a holder just above the bath when it's not in use.

Window: If your room has only a small window, you can afford to dress it with a gorgeous fabric, especially if making it into a Roman blind, which requires a minimal amount of material. The good-quality linen used to make this blind adds texture and pattern to the scheme but is fine enough to let plenty of light filter through.

Accessories: The dark wood cabinet cuts down on clutter by providing a home for toiletry supplies, and its barred, see-through doors help to keep them in sight and mind. Sisal and seagrass baskets supplement the natural textures in the room as well s providing storage for laundry and smaller items.

The look: You don't have to scatter shells everywhere to bring a breath of sea air into your bathroom. Blue and white, the colors of ocean, sky and surf, are all you need to create a marine feel, a theme hinted at in this room by the seagull print above the bath.

Color: Although blue is a cool color, deeper shades can create an inviting atmosphere. The blue on the wood panelling sets the tone for a warm, summery feel, while lighter shades on the upper walls and floor keep the overall effect bright and airy. The white suite stands out beautifully against the deep background, and crisply contrasts with the rich wood colors of the toilet seat and cabinet, which add a strong air of tradition to the scheme.

Wood panelling: The tongue-and-groove panelling on the lower walls has been fitted over old tiles, avoiding the tedious job of removing them.

If you want to attempt a similar cover-up, add wide wooden beading along the top of the panels to conceal the tile edges and give a neat finish.

Suite: The suite enhances the room's comforting traditional atmosphere – its classic style is denoted by angular lines and curved moldings, a mahogany-effect toilet seat and old-fashioned pillar tap knobs. The tub is panelled with tongue-and-groove painted in the same shade as the upper walls.

Accessories: Metallic accessories echo the gleaming chrome taps: the toothbrush holder and toilet roll holder add sparkle and shine, while a curly wire magazine rack provides a home for reading matter beside the loo. The dark wood storage cabinet and decorative wall lamps add to the traditional elements in the room.

The look: Imagine you're bathing in a country stream as you lie back and watch fish leaping around you or feast your eyes on the natural greens and browns of leaves and bark. Country house elegance takes on the great outdoors in this original scheme.

Color: A blend of greens, greys and wood tones recreates that woodland feel. The emphasis is on natural materials, including the dark grey marble flooring, wood-effect bath panelling and natural-fiber rug. The deep pine greens of the chair and lower wall decoration tone with the flooring. On the upper part of the walls, pale green sets a more refreshing mood, teaming up with the white ceiling and splashback to keep the overall look light and airy. A richly patterned blind adds definition to the window and echoes accents of russet and yellow introduced in accessories.

Walls: Stencils and paint

effects add plenty of interest to the walls. The lower section is decorated with a jade green marbled effect that echoes the flooring. Applied in blocks, it mimics the panelled walls of an old country house. Above this, a lively border of stencilled fish motifs runs around the room, while a more subtle design outlines the top of the walls. Whatever your room theme, specialist stencil companies are almost certain to stock a motif that suits it, and can also supply the paints and brushes to apply it.

Accessories: The theme of fishy goings-on continues with the quirky shelf brackets, which reflect the shape of the stencil motif. Pile on rustic texture in mats, pots, sponges and loofahs. For extra outdoor authenticity, add items that come straight from the natural world, such as plants and pieces of driftwood.

The look: Boat designs on pictures and fabrics, along with a bright and breezy color scheme, give this bathroom its jaunty nautical air – just what you need to set your sails flapping first thing in the morning.

Color: Deep turquoise and dazzling white make an invigorating combination. Balancing them equally allows the clean white splashback tiles and suite to counteract the richness of the turquoise walls and bath panel, giving the overall look a refreshing feel. The dark blue background of the window blind also forms a vibrant contrast with the turquoise and makes an effective foil for its jazzy boat motifs in primary colors. Its border echoes the sandy tones of the carpet.

Suite: A close-coupled toilet, with no connecting pipe separating the tank and bowl, has a neat appearance. Boxing in the pipework alongside and continuing the white tiling over its housing also gives the room a shipshape look. Unfussy wooden bath panelling, painted to match the walls, adds to the room's casual country character.

Window: Although soft furnishing features in a bathroom are relatively limited, window dressings can play a key role in enhancing its theme or color scheme. A bold print works well at a wide window, and a simple Roman blind shows it off to advantage. Textured window panes guarantee privacy even when the blind is raised.

Accessories: Colorful boat and harbor pictures echo the blind design, and wide white frames lend them emphasis against the turquoise walls. The long windowsill offers plenty of space for a display of natural accessories: plants in terracotta pots conceal the central window frames, while pots of pebbles and shells underline the seaside theme.

The look: Box in a simple white suite with wood panelling, and you're halfway to creating a look that's pure country. Rustic wooden accessories, simple toiletries and jugs of fresh flowers complete the picture.

Color: Mellow yellow is the perfect choice for a cheerful country scheme – as well as evoking a sunny corn-meadow feel, it blends beautifully with natural wood tones. Using the same shade on all the woodwork creates a plain and simple backdrop for the numerous small accessories that contribute character to this look. The floorboards and the upper part of the walls balance the warmth of the yellow with a cool off-white, helping to maintain a feeling of space and height.

Suite: If modern fixtures look too functional for your taste, try a hide-and-disguise job with painted wood. Tongue-and-groove boards create a cosy, country-cabin look and make a low-cost, easy-to-fit covering for baths as well as walls. If you're a skilled woodworker, you could probably also build your own vanity unit around a sink. If not, try to find a local carpenter who can make one to your design. This traditional-style cupboard was created using MDF, plus ready-made panelled doors, which give access to storage space beneath the sink.

Accessories: Have fun with accessories if you like a homely look. Decorative items, such as the bird and ship ornaments, add individuality, while the framed postcards introduce a touch of nostalgia. Reinforce the rustic feel with driftwood frames, earthenware containers and simply packaged toiletries in natural colors. Shaker furnishings are great for any country scheme – the wooden rocking chair combines comfort with style, while a peg rail provides hanging space.

BATHROOM TIP
Pictures and ornaments give traditional-style bathrooms an inviting feel but make sure any treasured items will tolerate a steamy atmosphere. You can protect paintings or photos by framing them behind glass or Lucite

The look: A selection of brilliant pinks and yellows and a lively wallpaper patterned with bathroom bits and pieces create a bright, wide-awake look. Retro patterns and colors give the room a fun 1950s flavor but the streamlined wall-mounted suite brings it bang up to date.

Color: A wallpaper or fabric design can form a good starting point for a room scheme. If you choose to cover your walls with a busy or distinctive pattern, keep the rest of the decor simple – balancing it with a bold, plain color picked out from the design will create a striking impact. Hot pink forms a vibrant contrast for the white suite and floor tiles, and fitting the wooden boarding horizontally adds to the room's individual style.

Suite: Wall-mounted fittings give a particularly neat look, especially if they have clean,

contemporary curves and compact proportions. The toilet tank and other workings are hidden behind the wood panelling, and a half pedestal encloses pipework below the sink. The flush is operated by a discreet push-button control fixed into the ledge above the panelling. Choosing a wall-mounted suite means the toilet and bidet can be fixed at a height to suit you, and also makes it easier to clean the floor beneath. Taps with tall spouts are convenient for smaller fittings as they stand clear of the sink area.

Accessories: Many furnishing collections offer accessories such as bathrobes and laundry bags to match their wallcoverings or fabrics. Team these with plain towels, beakers and vases that contribute dashes of further color picked out from the wallpaper design.

BATHROOM TIP
Make sure that panelling fitted around fixtures can be easily removed to allow instant access to any boxed-in plumbing if it should need repairs

The look: White-painted wooden boarding, trelliswork door panels and leafy potted palms give this bathroom the airy elegance of a Victorian summerhouse. A big sink and marble countertops make it a place to luxuriate in.

Color: Wall-to-wall white creates a beautifully fresh feel, although it can look monotonous and clinical. This room counteracts that adverse effect by punctuating the white surfaces with textural pattern – the lines of the wood panelling on the walls and the trelliswork designs of the door fronts. These add plenty of interest so that additional color can be kept to a minimum. Only the subtle greys of the marble countertops and flooring, plus a few accents in plants and accessories, interrupt the expanse of pure white.

Suite: A rectangular sink with generous proportions has an air of traditional luxury that complements the styling of the room. The pillar taps also have classic-style controls. By contrast, the toilet's compact modern design makes it look neat and unobtrusive, especially with the tank concealed inside a wooden housing.

Fitted units: With cupboards built-in below and beside the sink, and on the wall, this bathroom enjoys plenty of storage space. The panelled and trelliswork doors exude classic elegance, but a similar look could be created quite cheaply. Use MDF to build the carcasses, then look for ready-made panelled doors – some kitchen companies sell these on their own, without units. Replace some of the inner panels with MDF trelliswork, available from DIY stores, then paint everything white before fitting the doors. More trelliswork has been used to make shutters for the windows and a cover for the radiator below the sill.

BATHROOM TIP
If you buy fixtures from different sources, make sure the pieces you choose are all a similar shade. Even whites can vary in tone, especially among older fittings

The look: A suite with unusual octagonal shaping is offset by equally distinctive decor in a room that brings a designer touch to rustic style. The natural grain and texture of wood plays a starring role, with the walls and window dressed with panels that look as if they've been hewn straight from the log.

Color: The glowing tones of the dramatic wood panelling give the room a warm and welcoming atmosphere, while the chocolate browns of the low wall and ceramic floor tiles lend the look a sophisticated feel. An absence of further color reinforces the impact of the woody browns and the smart simplicity of the scheme, although the black and white cow-print bag adds a quirky touch of modernity.

Suite: The suite brings traditional style into the 21st century. The fittings feature an octagonal outline with distinct lines and very flat, even surfaces, which work well in this modern environment. The sleek white fixtures are thrown into relief against the dark backdrop, which helps to show off their attractive shape.

Wooden furnishings: The wood panels used in this room were specially produced, but you could create a similar warm and natural effect by covering walls with planks of wood cut to different widths. You could also try dressing a window using sheets of wood veneer. Used for marquetry, and on furniture, they are so thin that light shines through them. Insert an eyelet in the center of each strip and hang from metal hooks at the top of the window. Complete the look with wooden furniture – whether modern or rustic, anything with beautiful grain will fit the bill.

The look: Wood, wicker and traditional furnishings create an inviting country look. An all-neutral scheme complements the room's rustic character but brings an air of restrained elegance to cottage style – there are no clichéd chintzy florals here.

Color: Walls with a pale neutral colorwash and oak floorboards with a grey wax finish create a smart but relaxing foil for the warmer tones of the wicker baskets and honey-colored bath panels. With walls covered in a stylishly patterned woodland-inspired paper, the adjoining toilet forms a cosy enclave off the main bathroom. Country-style checks make a subtle appearance as white and taupe splashback tiles around the bath.

Walls: The combination of wallpaper and paint adds interest to the scheme, while choosing similar tones for both gives the adjoining rooms a unified look. If you want a busily patterned paper in a small room but fear that it might overwhelm the space, look for a design with just two colors. The bathroom walls are painted using shades that match the wallpaper – a mixture of artist's acrylics in raw umber, grey and yellow ochre applied as a colorwash using scumble glaze.

Suite: The suite combines clean lines with the substance and shape of a traditional design. The pine-effect finish of the toilet seat and the classic-style bath panelling makes it perfect for a country cottage look. The distinctive curves of the sink rim are complemented by an arched splashback molding, echoed by the rim of the toilet tank.

Accessories: Wicker baskets and handpainted Spanish jugs enhance the country look, while framed prints add manor-house chic. A wooden table with a distressed paint finish combines storage capacity with character.

BATHROOM TIP
Adding scumble glaze to a colorwash helps to stop diluted paint becoming too weak and runny. It increases the paint's working time, making it easier to achieve the effect you want. Buy it at craft shops or specialist paint stores

The look: Sunlight filtering through white-painted shutters highlights the small gold squares of the wallpaper and the sleek curves of the suite in this scheme that combines elements of colonial style with contemporary glamour.

Color: A neutral palette bridges the gap between contemporary and colonial as it is a popular choice for both decorating styles. The calming mid-tone background of the wallpaper tones harmoniously with the wooden flooring while providing a warm foil for the white suite and shutters. Its reflective gold squares have a fashionable luminous sheen but also suggest a latticework effect reminiscent of ethnic-style screens. The darker shades of natural accessories add depth to the look.

Suite: The sculptural curves of the suite and the streamlined single-lever taps establish the mood of contemporary chic. The wall-mounted sink is particularly neat, all pipework concealed within its half-pedestal. Discreet Lucite splashbacks protect the wallpaper while letting its design show through. The clear panels are fixed in place with chrome-capped mirror screws.

Floor: Combining trendy looks with tropical overtones, the deck flooring is a clever and effective way of covering a concrete sub-floor. Made from natural teak, it is warm to the touch and develops a beautiful patina as it ages. Simple mats in natural colors help to make it more homey.

Accessories: The louvred shutters and smaller furnishings introduce the truly colonial elements of the look. When the shutters are open, bamboo plants on the balcony offer a screen of privacy with an oriental look. The rattan trunk, basket platter and dark wood mirror frame offset the clean white suite with natural color and texture, plus decorative country-style design.

BATHROOM TIP
If you like a patterned look but can't face hanging wallpaper, use a rubber stamp to print motifs on plain painted walls. It's quick and easy to do, and DIY and craft stores offer a wide range of stamp designs

The look: A suite with traditional English styling brings an air of subtle elegance to a scheme inspired by Shaker design. Cool cream, warm wood and unfussy furnishings recreate the air of natural simplicity favored by early New England settlers.

Color: Cream forms part of the classic Shaker palette, and using it to cover the walls from floor to ceiling creates the calming atmosphere that their design philosophy demands. The white suite and splashback tiles provide a crisp contrast, while the wooden flooring and accessories inject natural warmth to give the pale scheme a welcoming feel.

Suite: The simple decor makes a plain foil for the more elaborate shaping of the suite. Its Edwardian design is based around angular edges and soft curves, with the sink splashback and tank rim featuring gently sweeping lines. The pedestals have the corners sliced off and are finished with stepped bases. Traditional chrome-plated taps continue the elegant look, but a plain glass panel makes an unobtrusive shower screen.

Floor: The natural grain and color of wooden flooring make it a popular choice for country-style settings. If you live in an older house, you may be lucky enough to find original floorboards hidden beneath carpet or linoleum. If they are in good condition, strip them back using sanding machines from a rental shop. (They come with instructions on how to use them.) Seal the sanded surface with floor varnish to prevent water from penetrating the wood.

Accessories: Fuss-free design, functionality and natural texture are key ingredients for Shaker accessories. A pegboard typifies the style and offers hanging space above the sink. The rustic basket below keeps spare towels handy.

The look: The combination of a traditional white suite, wood panelling and soft sage green walls gives this bathroom a period look that is understated but strong on style. The checkerboard floor design adds a distinctive touch.

Color: Pine panelling gives a country twist to this classic look. Its natural appeal is complemented by the restful sage green wall color and the light but warm neutral shade of the splashback tiles. With the room dominated by wood, the floor needed something to give it a lift. Painting it in a solid color would have unbalanced the look, but this checkerboard pattern adds plenty of character while preserving the beauty of its grain.

Panelling and suite: Classic-style wood panelling makes it easy to create a formal look in a characterless room, and is simple to fix onto walls or around a bath. The semi-recessed sink is built into a matching vanity unit made by a local carpenter, while a wood-effect seat ties the toilet into the scheme. Finish wooden surfaces with clear matte varnish to protect them from damp.

Floor: The checkerboard design has transformed an ordinary wooden floor into a stunning feature. To apply the design to sanded boards, first measure and mark out large blocks. Mask off alternate squares and paint these with woodstain in a walnut shade. When dry, remove the masking tape and apply clear floor varnish over the entire surface.

Accessories: Sheer cotton voile curtains give a more dressy look than blinds, and conceal an ugly window without blocking light. Other striking accessories include the mirror with Venetian glass frame and the brass wall sconces, which together create a grand focal point.

The look: Freshen up a small bathroom with a serving of spring greens. In this tiny space measuring just 6.5 x 8ft, a cool color scheme and some imaginative timberwork clear the way for streamlined contemporary style.

Color: Two shades of apple green give this room its up-to-the-minute appeal. In a restricted space, a simple scheme works best, with the room neatly divided into two blocks of color. Using the lighter shade above maintains an airy feel, and the white suite also keeps the mood fresh. The wooden grille covering the radiator allows the deeper green used on the wall panelling to continue all around the room. The checked blind adds a contrasting dash of dark blue, highlighting the crispness of the greens.

Suite: Fitting a standard-sized bath left little room for a toilet, but a slimline model slots neatly into the space available. With a design inspired by Art Deco style, it teams a curvaceous bowl with a chunky, angular pedestal.

Radiator cover: The radiator is concealed behind a timber screen, painted to match the wall panelling. Its grille lets heat through, and a rail fixed to the front allows the radiator to double as a towel warmer. The ledge along the top provides attractive display space. This cover was custom built, but off-the-rack MDF designs with fretwork fronts can be bought in flatpack form ready to paint.

Window: A double set of blinds makes for a versatile window dressing. The Roman blind can be lowered for complete privacy, whereas the Venetian blind allows finer control over light levels. The checked fabric plays an important role in adding color and pattern to the scheme.

BATHROOM TIP
No space for a radiator? Consider underfloor heating instead, especially if you are lucky enough to be starting from scratch

The look: You can almost hear the waves crashing on the shore in this refreshing beachhouse-style bathroom. Painted wooden boarding forms the basis of this simple look.

Color: A light shade of aqua is perfect for creating a cool, sea-fresh environment. Teamed with white-painted flooring, it makes the room feel as invigorating as a splash in the waves. A cream-colored suite complements the natural feel, while rustic accessories in dark wood and wicker add texture and depth.

Walls and floor: Tongue-and-groove planks pinned horizontally to the walls give the room a real beachhouse look. For a nautical appearance, paint the wood with several coats of thinned-down emulsion. The floor is painted with diluted white emulsion, which allows the grain of the boards to show through, giving a sun-bleached effect. Protect all wood surfaces in a bathroom with a coat of varnish.

Suite: With contemporary shaping enhanced by subtle detail, the suite would look at home in many different settings. While its clean curves offer simplicity, the stepped moldings around the edge of the sink and tank lid add a more decorative touch. Modern chromium-plated taps enhance its sleek style.

Accessories: Complete the look with natural objects – a mirror framed in driftwood, a weather-beaten stool and an assortment of shells and pebbles will all help to reinforce the seashore theme. Make a fitting display space by edging a shelf with a wavy MDF trim, painted in blue.

The look: A combination of robust blue and minty green creates a bold but refreshing color scheme for this modern bathroom. Boxing in the fixtures helps to give the small, narrow space a streamlined look, enhancing the air of contemporary cool.

Color: The bright blue tiles that run from the window to the sink form a vibrant block of color in contrast with the white fittings. The blue mood continues with a sparkly vinyl floorcovering, but painting the walls in a pale blue as well might have made the room feel too cold. Instead, a fresh minty green lifts the scheme.

Suite: Compact modern fittings economize on space. The back-to-wall toilet has its tiny tank hidden inside a framework, which forms a handy shelf for bath oils. To create further storage, the semi-recessed sink is surrounded by a vanity unit with tiled countertop. This unit, the bath surround and the toilet

housing were all built to order by a local carpenter.

Window: As the only source of natural light, the small window needs a dressing that will keep the room bright by day but provide privacy when required. A Venetian blind fits the bill, and this wooden design is stained a pale bluey-green, a perfect match for the walls.

Accessories: Smart chrome accessories, such as the toilet-brush holder and bath rack, set the seal on an up-to-the-minute scheme. The mirror above the sink incoporates a sleek shelf for toothpaste and brushes.

BATHROOM TIP
Not enough cash to splash on a suite? Update your old one by fitting slick modern taps, and invest in a matching set of well-designed chrome accessories to get your bathroom sparkling like a new pin

The look: Earthy autumnal shades bring a cosy glow to this high-ceilinged room. The simple storage unit and window blinds set a contemporary mood, and clever disguises make the existing suite blend in by hiding or replacing fussy design details.

Color: Tall rooms in old houses can feel chilly and uninviting, but a dose of warm color soon raises the temperature. To make a feature of the picture rail, the untiled wall is painted in three glowing colors: the main part in deep red, the rail a slightly darker shade and the space above in a pale ochre. These rich colors tone beautifully with the knotty pine flooring and skirting board. With plenty of warmth to balance it, the white-tiled wall has a freshening rather than chilling effect, and the earthy browns of the large painting soften it further.

Suite: Dated scallop detailing made the suite a real turn-off, so the curved bath panels have been replaced with painted tongue-and-groove boarding and the shell-shaped toilet seat swapped for a simple wooden one. A terrycloth cushion filled with washable stuffing conceals a scalloped ledge on the bath. Fixed in place with two suction cups, it acts as a headrest.

Storage: The small compartments of this CD rack are ideal for toiletries, and its adjustable shelving can accommodate items of varying sizes. Tall and slim, it requires little wall space, fitting neatly into the narrow area between two windows.

Windows: Plain white roller blinds score high on contemporary simplicity, and are cheap to buy. They also let plenty of natural light filter through, especially if made from fine cotton.

BATHROOM TIP
Although popular in the 1970s, colored suites are a definite no-no nowadays, so it's worth replacing them if you can afford to. Crisp white fittings will go with any decor, outlast fashion fads and could be a selling point if you put your home on the market

The look: If you're stuck with a suite in a color you hate but can't afford to change it, the answer is to decorate the rest of the room in shades that make it easier to live with.

Color: The outdated dark green suite in this bathroom had to stay, but a complete whitewash has freshened up the gloomy decor that surrounded it. White not only makes a small bathroom feel light and bright, but also goes with any other color, and creates a clean foil for dark or dull-colored fittings. This simple scheme plays up the contrast between the walls and suite with the addition of green accents in accessories.

Tiles: Why go to the trouble of removing old wall tiles? If all you want to do is change the color of plain, flat tiles, the easiest way is to paint them. Clean them thoroughly with sugar soap and allow to dry, then apply tile primer followed by a top coat of tile or gloss paint – applying it with a small roller will give an even finish. If you want to fit textured or patterned tiles, you can lay them over the old ones, using a wooden strip or pieces of tile to conceal the double thickness. Ensure that the original tiles are stuck firmly before you start.

Accessories: A set of simple wooden shelves, painted to blend in with the walls, allows for a display of accessories that add both color and character. Metallic items, such as the chrome Venetian blind, vases and candle sconces, not only complement the cool greens but also reflect light, making the tiny room feel even brighter.

The look: A flash of budget-wise brilliance brings a small bathroom right up to date. Red and purple introduce zingy color without overpowering the tiny space, while a few simple and inexpensive improvements give the existing suite a new lease of life.

Color: Basing a scheme on white increases the sense of space, but adding moderate amounts of vivid color will transform the look. A red and purple combination gives a funky modern feel. For maximum impact, use bold blocks of color; a small floor area can carry off a scarlet vinyl, while the window alcove provides a self-contained space for a splash of purple.

Suite: A white suite in good condition can be adapted to suit any decor. This bath's old brown panelling has been replaced with smooth white-painted MDF boards. The sink also enjoys cleaner lines, with an MDF housing which hides its

pedestal and creates storage space. The toilet tank is concealed behind a purple-painted box, and the toilet seat has been glammed up with red spray enamel, a pot of glitter and a few coats of polyurethane varnish.

Shower curtain: Make a shower curtain in the color of your choice using polyurethane-coated nylon. Measure from the rail to just above the bottom of the tub and cut two pieces this length, then sew them together lengthwise. Mark points at 6-8in intervals, 2.5cm from the top of the curtain. Using an eyelet kit, punch a hole and insert an eyelet at each marked spot. Hang from curtain rings.

The look: Make the smallest room in the house the most colorful – a lick of paint is the key to a low-cost makeover. Add a few decorative accessories to complete your dramatic transformation.

Color: Strong color will give a small bathroom a character boost. Mauve and aqua are both contemporary favorites but make an original combination that gives this room an individual look. Cool colors have a less cramping effect than warm, fiery ones, and using the lighter of the two shades on the upper part of the walls helps to maintain an airy atmosphere. Wood panelling can be painted in any color you like, and usually works out cheaper to buy and install than tiles.

Sink: The big rectangular sink has classic looks, which are complemented by traditional-style taps. Small fittings obviously give you more room to move in tiny bathrooms but larger ones can create an air of luxury. If your heart is set on a generously sized sink, measure up carefully to ensure that there's space for you to stand in front and lean over it comfortably.

Mirror: Large mirrors are excellent for brightening dark rooms, especially if positioned where they can reflect light from the window. They can also help to make a small room feel larger by reflecting the space itself. This unusual wavy design combines practicality with decorative style.

Accessories: The curves of the metal accessories echo the wavy lines of the mirror, from the modern chrome storage cart to the wall-mounted candleholder which gives the room an air of period charm. Towels continue the color theme, with a mix of shades from pale green and mauve to deep turquoise.

The look: With soft yellows suggesting sunshine and sand, and distressed cupboard doors reminiscent of weathered driftwood, this tiny bathroom has a seaside flavor. The built-in sink and fitted units create a ship's cabin feel.

Color: Yellow ensures a sunny atmosphere but, as a warm color, may make a small room feel tinier, so this scheme balances it with a splashback of fresh white tiles above the bath. Using similar yellows on the walls and cupboards gives the room a streamlined appearance, while the distressed doors create a comfortably lived-in look. Blue accents enrich the scheme by providing a vibrant contrast with the yellow.

Suite: A slipper-shaped bathtub, which narrows at one end, has improved access to this tiny bathroom. Fitting the semi-recessed sink into cupboard also makes efficient use of space. As well as creating storage, it provides a countertop around the sink and conceals its pipework to give a neater look.

Storage: Built-in cupboards maximize storage space in a small bathroom and are invaluable for keeping it neat and tidy. As a cost-effective option, ask a local carpenter to build some, then paint them to match the rest of your decor. For a distressed effect, first apply a dark shade then, when dry, rub candle wax over areas that might suffer wear, such as panel edges. Apply a lighter paint color and leave to dry, then rub with steel wool to expose patches of base coat.

Floor: As well as having natural good looks and being comfy underfoot, cork is one of the best-value floorcoverings. Buy unfinished tiles and coat with layers of cork tile sealant or hardwearing varnish to seal them for bathroom use.

The look: If you've inherited an all-white bathroom, it shouldn't cost much to smarten it up. You don't have to blast the walls with bright color – simple designs painted on tiles and flooring give this room its individual look, while clever storage solutions add color and character.

Color: A blend of subtle greens and greys takes the clinical edge off the white, creating a relaxed mood that suits the casual style of the furnishings. A mix of tones and textures adds interest – from the forest greens of the tile designs and floor stripes to the olive seersucker curtain and the metallic grey of the galvanized boxes.

Suite: If your budget won't run to an expensive vanity unit or swanky bath surround, why not improvise? Galvanized boxes hide unsightly pipes beneath the sink and provide serious storage capacity, while a seersucker curtain screens the space beneath the bathtub, which is also used for storage.

Splashback: Green alchemy symbols give a lift to these plain white tiles. If you want to paint tiles already on your wall, practice on spare ones first. Make sure the tiles are clean and dry, then decorate with simple designs using tile paint and an artist's brush.

Floor: Wavy stripes add pattern and color to the vinyl floor tiles. When decorating vinyl or linoleum, use a product formulated for these surfaces, as ordinary paints won't stick. For this effect, first paint the floor in cream. When dry, tear the edges off strips of wide masking tape and stick to the floor. Paint a darker shade between the strips. When dry, remove the tape.

BATHROOM TIP
If crumbling grout is spoiling the look of your tiles, remove it carefully using something pointed, such as an old screwdriver. Apply new grout with a small sponge. Work it in well, wipe off excess with a damp sponge, then polish when dry

The look: Choosing a budget suite and inexpensive tiling needn't mean skimping on style. Courageous use of color can add character to the humblest furnishings. This room gets a retro 1950s feel, with a scheme based on bold black and white.

Color: Big black and white tiles arranged in checkerboard patterns define the 1950s look, and painting the lower part of the wall black reinforces the color contrast. Chrome fittings, splashes of hot lipstick pink and a cool pistachio-green door all add to the retro style.

Suite: If you reckon you can't afford new fixtures, think again – this classic white suite was fairly inexpensive. Bathroom specialists often have budget collections and give good discounts in sales. You can get especially good deals on discontinued lines or ex-display models. Choose a simple white suite, then add your own style with the rest of the decor.

Tiles: Ceramic wall tiles and vinyl floor tiles in plain colors can be picked up cheaply, yet combining a couple of contrasting colors can create interesting effects. In this small room, a fully checkered splashback might have looked overpowering, but a two-tile-deep border of alternating black and white squares has plenty of impact.

Mirrors: The convex glass in the porthole-style mirrors offers a fish-eye view. The gilt frames have been sprayed with silver paint to match the chrome fixtures. These mirrors add to the room's character, while a small extendable model is a more practical addition above the sink.

The look: Painting the walls is the easiest – and cheapest – way to perk up a boring bathroom. If yours seems cold and uninviting, be adventurous – try a deep, warm pink to turn it into a cosy, alluring space.

Color: Passionate pink not only warms up this room but also gives it a luxurious atmosphere that suits the classic looks of the taps and fittings. The glamorous stone-effect patterning on the wood-panelled bath surround enhances this decadent air. White fittings and tiles set off the darker colors by providing a dazzling contrast.

Suite: The bath and sink have classic styling, with rectangular shaping and 1930s-style molding around the sink. A paint effect gives the wooden bath surround its stone-effect finish. The chrome-plated taps are also traditional in style, the bath/shower combo featuring a telephone handset.

Towel shelf: The unusual towel rack can be put together in minutes using a pair of white-painted shelf brackets and a few lengths of rope. Drill holes for the rope along the top of each bracket, and fix them to the wall. Then simply thread the rope through the holes and knot at each end to secure. The decorative brackets suit the classic feel of the room.

Mirrors: Mirrors serve more purposes in a bathroom than you might realize, adding decoration and interest to plain walls. Large mirrors are useful in small bathrooms because they reflect light and space, making the room appear bigger and brighter.

The look: Who says you can't afford a bright new bathroom? Crisp white tiles are amazingly cheap if bought in bulk, and you'll save loads of money if you buy a complete suite rather than individual pieces. Go-with-anything white gives you the freedom to change your color scheme at any time – simply splash on the paint.

Color: Brilliant colors not only create their own impact but also form a striking contrast with white. These fittings and tiles look fresh and clean against a sea of cool blue and bands of strong pink. The vertical panels of pink and white act like stripes, leading the eye upwards and adding height to the room.

Suite: The budget suite was cost-effective from a DIY store but, surrounded by clever color scheming and design, it looks the business. For a timeless contemporary look, choose fittings with clean lines and few fussy details, and remember that pure white will always be a winner. If you want to add color to your bath, build a surround of tongue-and-groove panelling, which you can paint or repaint to match your scheme.

Shelving: Galvanized shelves are sleek, chic and inexpensive. These show how shelving can be arranged creatively to form a stylish design feature. The short shelves add interest to the pink panels, helping them to make a focal point of the sink area.

Floor: Vinyl flooring is cheap, tough, easy to clean and comes in lots of great colors. Sold in sheet or tile form, it is also easy for anyone to lay. Matching the shade to the blue used on the walls boosts this room's color power even further.

BATHROOM TIP
Remember to budget for plumbing and electrical work – never attempt these jobs yourself. See the Advice section at the back of this book for professional bodies that can supply details of tradesmen in your area

The look: A smart monochrome color scheme establishes an air of city chic in this elegantly styled bathroom, where the classic good looks of the suite and fixtures are inspired by the Edwardian period.

Color: A combination of black and white is sure to set a distinguished tone. Glossy black wall tiles are offset by the crisp white walls and suite and light chromium taps, while the rich mahogany color of the toilet seat and bath panelling adds a touch of warmth. Elements of pattern give the look a decorative period feel: small black inset tiles enliven the floor area, while the wall tiles are topped off by a narrow border with a traditional geometric design. The grey and white stripes of the Roman blind continue the monochromatic scheme, with only the pictures and soap adding dashes of color.

Suite: Although the fittings show an Edwardian influence, they are not overfussy in appearance and are scaled to suit the size of modern homes. The sink has a bow front and generous rim, and its curves are echoed in the lid of the toilet tank. The classic-style taps and wood-effect toilet seat and bath panelling also evoke a traditional feel.

Window: Neater than curtains but providing an opportunity to introduce patterned fabric, a Roman blind is the perfect choice of window treatment for this smart but dressy scheme. Stripes work well with this type of blind as they complement the straight lines of the pleats. If you want to make a blind using your own fabric, look for a kit that includes all the fittings – it's easier than buying them separately and also provides full instructions.

BATHROOM TIP
A modern radiator detracts from the look of a period-style room, so seek out a traditional design. Specialist radiator companies and some bathroom suppliers stock them, or you could try junk yards for genuine period fittings

The look: Rustic simplicity meets classic splendor in this comfortable scheme, where a magnificent slipper bath makes a strong style statement amid a reassuring environment of unassuming colors and natural textures.

Color: Walls in soft cream, plus wood panelling painted in a gentle sage green, give this room its relaxed country feel, which is enhanced by the natural tone and texture of the seagrass flooring. Against this calming backdrop, the black and white coloring of the bath boldly asserts its classic contours and ensures that it is seen as a dramatic focal point.

Bath: With one end curving up to provide a luxurious headrest, a slipper bath makes an even more impressive sight than a standard roll-top. If you have the space, place it in the center of the room to show off its shapely lines and ornamental feet. As traditional freestanding baths have no surrounding surfaces, a bath rack is essential for holding soaps and washing items – look for one with a finish that matches your taps.

Floor: Seagrass and other natural floorcoverings create a comfortably rustic look, although their prickly fibers are not so kind to bare feet. Like normal carpeting, most types will not wear well in damp conditions, but can be used with care if backed with rubber. Coir matting is the most practical choice as its fibers benefit from being kept moist.

Accessories: The wall print and the selection of patterned tiles add touches of decorative detail while blending in with the subtle colors of the background. The white-painted wooden stool and towel rack have traditional country looks, and the leafy plant also adds to the natural feel.

The look: A mix of influences have had a hand in this cosy bathroom, which brims with decorative detail. Yellow checked wallpaper and a soft blue carpet create a comfortable country-house atmosphere, while Chinese-style plates and a Moroccan-inspired alcove add a more exotic touch.

Color: The yellow and white checks of the wallpaper fill the room with cheerful pattern and sunny color, creating a fresh, country feel. Blue enriches the scheme by forming a vibrant contrast. Choosing a deep-colored carpet adds a sense of comfort to the room, while using blue to pick out the alcove focuses attention on its shape. Color unites accessories as varied as the Moroccan lantern and oriental plates, which all feature similar shades of blue.

Suite: The distinctive scalloped detailing of the suite strikes a chord with the room's decorative character, while the wood tones of the maple-effect bath panelling and toilet seat enhance its country charm. The classic pillar taps are chromium plated.

Storage and display: The alcove provides an eye-catching display space. Its arched shape and intricately patterned shelf edgings point to Moroccan inspiration, perhaps suggested by the beaten metal lantern. The shelf trims are flat MDF moldings, available from good timber merchants in a range of patterns. They are glued in place and painted in a lighter shade of blue to make them stand out against the background. The wall around the recess is edged with braid, glued on and decorated with small chair studs. The blue and white plates have been arranged in a shape that echoes the arch of the alcove, with the pot given pride of place on a painted wooden corbel in the center.

BATHROOM TIP
Choose a vinyl wallpaper for a bathroom. Vinyl finishes are designed to withstand damp and condensation, so will last longer than other papers

The look: Purify your senses in a bathroom designed to wash the day away. Powdery pastels have just enough color power to refresh a sleepy mind. Together with a sculptural suite, flowing fabrics and ice-cool flooring, they create a totally cleansing environment.

Color: Pale but interesting shades are what gives this beautifully feminine scheme its character. Choose colors rather than bland neutrals, but maintain a light touch, with cool grey-green and ice-blue for walls and floor, and pretty pinks and yellows for other furnishings and towels. Areas of shine and sparkle in glass and Lucite accessories help to create a feeling of space and light. The vinyl flooring, which resembles tiny squares of glass, also has a shimmering, reflective quality that enhances the bright, clean feel of the scheme.

Bathtub: The old-fashioned elegance of the furnishings prevents the look from feeling overly clinical. The pink-painted roll-top bath, with elaborate feet picked out in white, looks twice as glamorous when draped with a flowing shower curtain. Hung from an oval rail fixed to the ceiling, the yellow curtain is deliberately overlong so that it swirls lavishly across the floor.

Sink: A painted consoletable with graceful curved legs serves as a washstand for the bowl-style sink, which is a modern take on a Victorian design. The taps are wall-mounted onto a splashback of hexagonal mosaic tiles.

Accessories: A Lucite shelf stacked with mock medical vessels in clear glass boosts the hygiene appeal, while a decorative candle chandelier sets a more romantic mood. A laundry bag in a pink and yellow floral print makes a pretty hideaway for bits and pieces not smart enough to put on show.

The look: A mood of cool restfulness pervades this room, thanks to cloudy blue-washed walls complemented by floaty sheer curtains and the graceful details of a classic-style suite and splashback.

Color: The blue colorwash is a beautifully subtle way of filling the room with color while maintaining a light and airy feel. Its shades are echoed by the splashback tiles, where soft blue inset and border tiles form a gentle contrast to the plain white squares. The natural wood tones of the flooring, bath panel and toilet seat help to warm up the cool scheme, while ceramics in intense blues strengthen it with accents of exotic Mediterranean color.

Suite: Fancy stepped moldings around bowl and pedestal bases give the suite its classic looks, while the wood-effect toilet seat and bath panelling also denote traditional style. The taps feature easy-to-use lever controls with a period design.

Splashback: Laying plain tiles diagonally gives them an individual look, and these have small blue insets to add further decorative interest. The border of blue pencil tiles provides definition between the white splashback and pale colorwash, and evokes a period feel by mimicking a dado rail.

Radiator: Despite adding warmth and comfort, modern radiators often have a cold, functional appearance. Painting them in a color can help; use radiator paint or apply multi-surface primer beneath a gloss or eggshell top coat. Ensure the radiator is cold before you start.

The look: Soak away your cares amid the genteel atmosphere of an Edwardian bathroom, as you gaze up at your art collection from the comfort of a hand-painted roll-top bath!

Color: The scheme is inspired by the colors of the bathtub, which is painted with a Florentine design in cobalt blue and golden yellow. The lighter blue that covers the walls has an uplifting, summery feel but is intense enough to make an impact in this high-ceilinged room. The smooth wooden flooring tones with the yellow to add warmth, while the white woodwork, suite and curtains provide a fresh contrast for the deeper colors.

Suite: The roll-top bath is a newly manufactured interpretation of a traditional design. A large freestanding bath like this requires space to show off its impressive curves so, if possible, place it in the center of the room to form a dramatic focal point. The sink, toilet and bidet would fit most rooms; although they have the lines of traditional fired clay fittings, they are contemporary in scale and proportion. Gold-plated taps and a mahogany-effect toilet seat enhance their elegant looks.

Window: White lace is a sure winner if you want a touch of old world charm, and will give your windows a beautifully dressed look without shutting out light. Make it into gathered curtains, and tie back loosely at the sides for a look of pure indulgent romance.

Accessories: Don't save paintings and ornaments for bedrooms and living rooms – a period-style bathroom does justice to sumptuous accessories. Search antique stores for decorative mirrors, and don't worry if the frames are slightly battered – they will add a fashionable air of shabby chic.

BATHROOM TIP
A large cast-iron tub can be very heavy when filled with water and bathers, so check before investing in one that your floor will be able to take the strain

The look: The original 1930s tiles on the walls inspired a slightly Art Deco flavor for this smart bathroom. An abundance of white keeps the mood bright and airy, while traditional fittings and checkerboard floor tiles add to the period feel.

Color: Decorating both the walls and ceiling in white creates a clean and sparkling atmosphere as well as a fantastic sense of space. Light bounces off the white surfaces, especially the glossy wall tiles, to make the room seem bigger and brighter. This plain, pale background lends greater impact to the period elements of the room – the narrow strips of green 1930s tiling stand out against the sea of white, while the bold black and white tiles put the focus firmly on the floor.

Suite: A suite with straight lines, angular shaping and traditional-style taps is in tune with the 1930s feel. The deep bath is boxed in with wooden panels: the long one features a raised design reminiscent of Art Deco patterns, while the hinged end panel opens like a door to allow space inside to be used for storage.

Mirrors: Set way up on the walls, the long mirrors may be a bit too high for comfortable use, but their prime purpose is to make the room feel wider by reflecting light and space. Placing two directly opposite each other is particularly effective. The small extendable mirror wall-mounted above the sink serves for shaving or applying cosmetics.

Towel rack: With a gleaming chrome finish that matches the taps, the simple towel rack is positioned just above the radiator so that its heat keeps the towels warm and dry.

The look: The Romans made a cult of bathtimes, so borrow a bit of their design style for a bathroom full of classical chic. Mosaic-effect flooring and splashback tiles handpainted with large Roman numerals set the theme.

Color: Plain cream walls and textured floor tiles in a similar shade suggest the sun-bleached surfaces of a Roman villa, and give the large room a wonderfully bright and airy atmosphere. Picking out the woodwork and shelves in white helps to enhance the richness of the cream, giving it a softer feel, while the golden glow of the taps and other fixtures introduces a hint of glamour. Orange border tiles add interest to the large floor area and characterful detail to the scheme, with their pattern based on an original Romanesque rope design.

Suite: A roll-top bath with elaborate sculptural feet, a sink with a pillar-like pedestal and an old-fashioned toilet with a high-level tank have classic good looks the Romans would have appreciated. The flush pipe and pull chain of the toilet have a gleaming brass finish that matches the taps.

Accessories: The glitzy golden highlights continue with a classy set of practical accessories, including toothbrush holders, a wall-mounted shelf and towel hooks and a stunning round mirror frame. A themed look relies on details to make it work and, like the numerals painted on the splashback tiles, the classic-style shelf corbels give a definite nod towards Roman style. These three shelves also offer a display area for evocative accessories such as a plaster head and pillar.

The look: Regency stripes get an up-to-date twist with fresh, invigorating colors, unleashing a burst of modern energy in a room based around a traditional-style suite and accessories.

Color: While the jazzy pattern and enlivening colors of the stripes create a refreshing atmosphere, the glossy white tiles and glass shower screen brighten the look even further by reflecting light from the window. Green towels and cream-colored candles echo the colors of the stripes.

Walls: The wall stripes are deliberately uneven, their slightly wavy edges giving a less regimental effect than clean-cut lines. First paint the entire wall with cream, then measure out the stripes and mark them on lightly with pencil, using a plumbline to get them straight. Paint on the green stripes freehand, using an artist's brush for the narrow ones. It doesn't matter if your coverage is slightly uneven as this will only add to the casual, contemporary effect.

Suite: Boxing in the bathtub with clean white tiles plays down the classic character of the suite, but it makes itself felt through details such as the wood-effect toilet seat and gold-plated taps. The shower head is also traditional in style; if you choose a fixed head like this, make sure you place it at the correct height so that all family members can stand upright beneath it. You will also need a shower screen to catch splashes – this glass model features a decorative etched design.

Towel racks: Two towel racks provide ample hanging space. A simple gold-plated bar allows towels to hang over the radiator, while a freestanding wooden rack also keeps them warm and dry when placed in front of it.

The look: A Victorian roll-top bath teams up with pretty painted bowls and other decorative accessories to create a bathroom with an air of old-fashioned charm. A restrained neutral color scheme sets the scene.

Color: Rustic stone flooring and wood-panelled walls painted in a rich cream give the room a traditional country-cottage feel. The cool blue-grey paintwork on the bath sets a slightly more sophisticated tone, while enhancing the relaxing atmosphere.

Wall panelling: Wood panelling is a popular choice of wall cover for classic or country-style bathrooms, and is ideal for concealing the less-than-perfect surfaces often found in older homes. Tongue-and-groove boards, widely available from DIY stores, are easy to install and can be painted in a color that matches your scheme. After painting, apply clear matte varnish to make the boards water-resistant, as damp can cause the wood to warp.

Suite: For any bathroom that aims to evoke classic comfort, a roll-top bath is a necessity. These large, cast-iron tubs originated in the nineteenth century but many bathroom dealers now offer authentic-looking, lightweight reproductions. This room's taps and small round wash sink also have a period look.

Accessories: Further old-fashioned glamour is added by the gilt-framed mirror and the chandelier reflected in it. Ceramic bowls decorated with pink and yellow flowers add accents of brighter color.

The look: Wallow in nostalgia with a look that's pure Art Deco. Patterned tiles and polished chrome fittings set the style for this flamboyantly luxurious bathroom, while photos and ornaments in the style of the era add perfect finishing touches.

Color: Pale lavender walls provide a chic backdrop for an otherwise monochrome scheme. A border of tiles at picture rail height adds classic proportions to the room, and the cream paintwork on the wall above echoes the floor tiles, which are enlivened by small black inserts. The Art Deco designs of the wall tiles are a key element in defining the look, and their jazzy patterns are offset by the plain black bath surround. A few pale green towels and floral-print accessories add subtle color accents to soften the angularity of the scheme.

Suite: The geometric shape of this sleek suite lends itself to Art Deco style, and the chrome-plated taps also evoke a retro feel. The black bathtub panel creates a smart contrast with the white fittings.

Wall tiles: You don't need many patterned tiles to make a style statement, so it's worth spending a bit more on luxurious designs that really say what you want them to. Distinctive tiles like these are best used sparingly – just one or two rows as a splashback above tub or sink will get the message across.

Accessories: The Art Deco influence continues with slick and shapely chrome accessories, such as the oval mirror and round wall lamps. The lithe, energetic bathing girls portrayed in the ornament and prints encapsulate the feelgood factor of the era.

The look: Classic chic gives a nod to contemporary cool, with a traditionally styled suite and flowing curtains looking to the past, while a steely combination of dark greys and white join with shiny chrome accessories to add a striking modern edge.

Color: This monochrome scheme sets a smart and sophisticated tone, and the grey paint shades complement the metallic gleam of the chrome furnishings. Dark grey walls could easily overwhelm a small room, but when balanced with plenty of fresh white they create a striking impact in this large, light-filled space. Using two shades as wall stripes introduces a subtle touch of tonal variation to soften the strident white and grey contrast.

Walls: Stripes in closely toning shades add interest to an extensive wall area and help to break up the intensity of the color without lessening its impact. Vertical stripes are also useful for increasing the illusion of height in a room. To get them straight, hang a plumbline from the top of the wall and mark on the stripes with pencil lines. Use low-tack tape to mask off each color, and let the paint dry before removing it to ensure a clean edge.

Suite: Fittings with classic styling give the room its air of old-fashioned chic. The curves of the roll-top bath are echoed by the rounded front and pedestal of the basin. Painting the bath to match the walls links the two strongest features of the look.

Accessories: Long sheer curtains add another classic touch to soften the scheme, but are plain enough to complement more modern elements such as the sleek storage cabinet and other chrome fittings which fill the room with high-shine glamour.

BATHROOM TIP
Although sheer curtains provide privacy by day, they won't preserve your modesty when the lights go on after dark. Add a roller blind, fitted within the window recess, which can be concealed behind a decorative heading when rolled up

The look: Old-fashioned fixtures and silver-painted floorboards bring an air of subtle glamour to this small bathroom, while accessories lend the look an oriental flavor.

Color: The walls are covered in a colorwash-effect paper in a pale neutral shade, which creates a light but calming backdrop for the small space. White woodwork and fittings freshen the overall look, while shiny silver floorboards also help to brighten up the room and increase the feeling of space by reflecting light. Their luxurious sheen is echoed by the gleam of the chrome-plated taps. The window blind and leafy plant offset the pale colors with darker accents of brown and green.

Suite: The plain white finish of the roll-top bath suits the simple styling of the room, while its gold-painted feet add just a hint of decadence. Its traditional looks are complemented by the chunky pedestal sink, with its classic square lines and molded detailing. The taps and telephone-style shower nozzle are also traditional in design.

Floor: While a glitzy paint effect might look overdone if used to cover the walls, a small floor area can add just the right amount of sparkle to glam up a tiny room. To give wooden floorboards a silvery finish, apply a metallic paint or multi-purpose enamel that's suitable for use on wood. When dry, protect the paintwork with two coats of floor varnish for a durable, waterproof surface.

Accessories: The bamboo ladder, woven paper blind and exotic potted palm all add character by introducing a touch of oriental style. The ladder not only looks decorative but also makes an excellent towel rail.

The look: A freestanding bath draped with shower curtains is the focal point of this romantically elegant Georgian-style scheme. Decorated in watery greens, with floral fabrics and gleaming gold accessories, this bathroom is unashamedly luxurious but also perfectly practical.

Color: If you want a room that's both colorful and relaxing, go for green. A soft shade creates a reassuring feel but also makes a refreshing foil for rich gold details and floral designs. Painting the walls above the picture rail in cool cream also maintains an airy atmosphere. A darker green adds definition to the bath, while a neutral carpet provides a calming base.

Suite: The bath and console sink have beautifully old-fashioned looks but are recent manufactures. Whereas genuine period pieces often require restoration, brand-new lookalikes combine modern quality with classic character.

Like original designs, the bath is made of cast iron. You can paint the white base in any color to match your scheme, and a touch of gold leaf will give the claw feet a glitzy finish.

Taps and shower: The taps also combine modern technology with traditional style, their brass finish complementing the room's gold accessories. The swan-necked shower riser and fixed head provide a more thorough soak than a hand-held mixer attachment, and long, gathered shower curtains add to the scheme's air of romance.

Accessories: Go all out for glamour with gilded accessories, such as the towel rack, candlestick and mirror frame. Or, if you find their lavish leaf and flower designs a bit too ornate, add a lighter touch of romance using pretty perfume bottles, a jug of fresh flowers and white cotton towels with a hint of embroidery.

BATHROOM TIP
Glam up wooden mirror frames and the claw feet of baths using a gilding kit, available from craft stores. It includes metallic leaf to give a golden finish, plus the glue and tools required to apply it

The look: A suite with sassy angles and a color scheme based on soft sea shades brings flirty 1930s style to a standard-sized bathroom. Subtle use of Art Deco patterns and accessories helps to create the look without overpowering the room.

Color: With a splashback of white tiles, and a pale shade of aqua adding the merest hint of color to the walls, the pale backdrop keeps the room feeling light and spacious, forming a cool foil for the stronger colors of the features that give it character. The flooring grounds the scheme with a sharper green, and helps draw attention to the Art Deco border tiles by echoing one of their colors. Black accents smarten up the look, and a striking green frame makes a focal point of the mirror.

Suite: The angular lines of the toilet and sink are reminiscent of the geometric patterns associated with Art Deco style. The bath carries a more direct reference, with the design on its panelling specially cut to echo the fan motif of the border tiles. The chrome-plated taps feature up-to-date lever controls but with traditional styling.

Floor: The floor is tiled with Marmoleum, a healthy, eco-friendly covering made from natural raw materials. Available in many colors and designs, it has a smooth surface that stops dirt and water from penetrating and discourages house dust mites.

Accessories: Sparkling chrome and glass accessories are a must for 1930s glamour. The sleek storage trolley displays a good-sized shaving or make-up mirror and a set of antique perfume bottles from that era, while the wall lamps that flank the mirror are also authentic Art Deco pieces.

The look: In this light, elegant scheme, an elaborately styled suite and glamorous gold accessories benefit from an ultra-simple background. With the walls and flooring kept perfectly plain, they work their own magic to create a romantic but classy look.

Color: Cream provides a versatile, space-enhancing backdrop for many styles of decor. Some people feel reluctant to team a white suite with cream walls, but they work well together as the contrast makes the cream feel richer and warmer, while boosting the fresh, clean appeal of the fittings. The pale blue paint of the bath injects a dash of subtle color, while the wooden flooring and furniture add a comforting touch of natural warmth.

Suite: If you like the idea of a romantic bathroom, have fun with fittings and search out the fanciest you can find. Although roll-top baths are now widely available, a highly decorative sink may be more difficult to track down. However, you could try adding white-painted trelliswork panels to the sides of a large traditional design. A toilet with high-level tank completes the old-fashioned line-up, while the gold-plated flush pipe and taps add a feeling of opulence.

Furniture: If you've space for it, occasional furniture will give a bathroom a comfier, lived-in look. This simple wooden chair and table provide a contrast in style that helps to highlight the ornate design of the suite.

Accessories: Wall-mounted accessories keep sink tops clear of clutter, add attractive finishing touches and give a bathroom a well-equipped feel. Look for fittings that match your taps – the shelf brackets, soap dish and tumbler holders enhance this room's luxurious golden glimmer.

The look: Black and white tiling combines a Victorian bathhouse feel with the impact of a bold modern color scheme. An eclectic mix of old and new furnishings reflects the two sides of its character – from the traditional roll-top bath to contemporary glass shelves and groovy rubber flooring.

Color: Black and white is not a relaxing combination for rooms where you spend a lot of time, but in a bathroom it can look smart and striking, and is a classic choice if you want a more masculine style. Big checkerboard wall tiles and black flooring make a dramatic statement. To soften the starkness of the monochrome scheme, the bath is painted in a warmer chocolate brown and the upper walls in a light mustard. The picture lifts the look with small splashes of brighter color – it's made up of pieces of towel glued to white cardboard.

Suite: The roll-top bath has traditional shaping but relatively simple feet, and, painted in a business-like brown, fits in well with the somewhat austere appeal of the room. The sink combines cleaner, more contemporary lines with classic-style taps.

Storage: The old cart has the practical plus points of a contemporary storage system – deep trays with plenty of space for towels and toiletries, and castors that make it easy to wheel around. Its battered metal finish forms a relaxed contrast with slick modern storage features such as the glass shelf and galvanized box.

Floor: Rubber flooring is fashionable, hardwearing and water-resistant, and this studded design provides an anti-slip surface. It is available in sheet or tile form in many different colors, but is more expensive than vinyl or linoleum.

The look: Recreate the feel of an old Italian villa using easy-to-achieve paint effects and characterful fixtures. With sun-baked browns, olive greens and wooden shutters, all you need is a ray or two of Tuscan sunshine to complete the picture.

Color: The earthy terracotta on the walls and the rich reddish-brown floor tiles create a warm glow, especially when bathed in sunlight from the window. The heat is tempered by a mix of cool but traditional greens, from the deep jade of the chair to the soft olive used on all the woodwork.

Paint effects: A terracotta colorwash gives the walls a natural, textural appearance. Apply a pale color, such as cream, and leave to dry. Then dilute a terracotta shade with water until you get the strength you want, and apply using a wide brush and crisscross strokes. The distressed effect on the wood panelling and shutters evokes an air of faded grandeur. First paint the wood with a terracotta shade, then rub candlewax over areas that might suffer wear, such as panel edges. Add a coat of light green, then, when dry, rub back with steel wool to expose patches of the base coat.

Suite: Any fixtures that look as if they have a history would sit well here. The farmhouse-style sink, with its decorative spray of ivy leaves, fits in perfectly with this classic country style, and a wood-clad tank gives the loo an individual look.

Window: Shutters give the room a continental appearance. This window is dressed with solid panels that fold back neatly to let in maximum light. The shaped pediment that tops the window adds an ornate finishing touch.

The look: This laid-back look exudes an air of faded glamour, with a mixture of old furniture and a tarnished gold paint effect on the bath. Off-white walls and painted floorboards form a serene backdrop.

Color: A mix of soft neutrals and natural textures creates a comfortable atmosphere, and using the same shade on the walls and floor makes for a particularly relaxing look. The matte gold finish on the tub tones with the gentle browns of the wooden furniture. The cream chest blends with the walls and floor while adding interest with subtle woven texture. Green and blue accents, featuring in the stool seat, book cover and bath design on the mirror, introduce the merest hint of color.

Bathtub: The roll-top bathtub came from a junk yard, which was full of original fixtures rescued from period homes.

See your local phone book to find your nearest yard. As long as an old bath is in good condition, you can decorate it to suit your scheme – the outside of this one has been spruced up with a mixture of gold powder and matte varnish, which gives an aged, tarnished finish. Gold-plated taps complete the glamorous transformation.

Furniture: Old furniture adds character to a bathroom and can be just as functional as purposely designed modern pieces. This room is home to a medley of antique store finds. The Lloyd Loom chest with padded lift-up lid doubles as a comfy seat and laundry basket. Every bathroom needs a mirror, and a classic design propped casually on a stool suits this lived-in look. The bathtub motif on its top panel adds the perfect finishing touch.

BATHROOM TIP
Don't keep wooden furniture too near tubs and sinks as water splashes can damage waxed surfaces. Give it a good polish to protect it from the steamy bathroom atmosphere

The look: If there's always a line for the bathroom in the mornings, decorate with bright red. It stimulates a sense of urgency, so will get people in and out fast. This room offsets its striking color scheme with more traditional fixtures and furnishings.

Color: A strong scarlet used as a flat, solid wall color is sure to make an impact. Teaming it with plenty of white prevents it from overwhelming a small room, and also adds extra energy by creating a dazzling contrast. Here red and white are equally balanced, with both colors used on the walls and then played off against each other in a more lively fashion in the checkerboard floor tiles. Yellow accents help to temper the strong contrast while adding a third cheerful color to the mix.

Sink: The flowing curves of the pedestal sink are easy on the eye, a shapely contrast with the bold geometric effect of the floor tiles. Tall pillar taps complement its classic styling.

Furniture: The white-painted wooden drawer also features elegant curved detailing, and the wooden chair adds a relaxed natural touch amid the strong colors. While the open shelves of the drawer unit keep toiletries and towels easily accessible, a family bathroom also needs a wall-mounted cabinet, preferably with lockable door, to keep medicines out of reach of small children.

Floor: Combining vinyl or linoleum tiles in different colors is an easy way of adding enlivening pattern to your bathroom. Vinyl is easy to lay, but make sure that the floor surface is even before you start. Linoleum is more expensive than most vinyls and should be laid by a professional fitter.

The look: Dark wood panelling set amongst simple white walls gives this bathroom the air of a traditional gentleman's club. A suite with distinctive rope-design moldings sets the seal on the look of sophisticated grandeur.

Color: The rich color of the solid cherrywood flooring and the darker tones of the mahogany-effect bath panel give the room a warm, comfortable atmosphere, while contrasting them with plain white walls keeps the look clean and unfussy. The set of monochrome pictures in simple black frames enhances the smart, masculine feel, and any additional color accents are limited to neutral shades, such as the camel-colored towel.

Suite: The rope-twist molding around the bathtub and column-like pedestals, and the arch rim detail on the sink give this suite its distinctive traditional looks. The taps feature an interesting mixture of chromium and light-gold finishes.

Wall panelling: The panelled effect on the wall behind the bath has been created using strips of MDF, which are decorated with a wood-effect paint technique in a color that matches the flooring. DIY stores and craft shops stock graining kits which include the paints and tools you need to create a convincing wood grain finish. These panels frame a large mirror, which helps to increase the illusion of space.

Accessories: The gallery of photographs adds personality to this simple scheme, and their subject matter – portraits of film stars – injects an air of glamour. Arranging them side by side around the walls not only breaks up the expanse of plain white but also adds a sense of order to the room.

The look: As this room shows, color and creative accessorizing can pull even the tiniest bathroom out of the doldrums. An unusual mix of mellow shades sets the mood for an offbeat look, while decorative accessories and shelving add character.

Color: With warm yellow offset by cool mauve and fresh aqua, none of the key colors is strong enough to overpower the tiny space, but they create a lively look when used together. More color is included as accents – in the deep pink and orange towels and the lime green candles. The flowers of the shower curtain echo the wall colors.

Mosaic tiles: Ideal for creating a trendy splashback, mosaic tiling can help to bring a jaded bathroom back to life. To make it easy to cover large areas, mosaic tiles can be bought attached to backing sheets. Apply adhesive to the tiled side and stick to the wall. When dry, carefully peel off the backing sheet and grout the tiles in the normal way.

Shelves: You don't need expensive built-inx cupboards to keep your bathroom tidy. The trelliswork shelving units fit in well with the mood of the room and look pretty even when packed with run-of-the-mill toiletries, yet they were a bargain buy from a local shop.

Accessories: Treat your bathroom as you would any other room in the house, by adding character with pictures and ornaments. Decorative items and a collection of candles add to the relaxed, romantic feel of this room.

The look: If you want to achieve that sea-fresh feeling, you can't go wrong with cool blues. A few colored furnishings against a backdrop of white are all that's needed for a shipshape modern look.

Color: A fail-safe method of room scheming is to use a single color in many different shades, from light to dark, throughout your room. This idea works particularly well with blues, which need only the addition of white to lift the look. In this room, white is used in abundance to create a fresh atmosphere, while the blues feature in smaller amounts – from the navy flooring to the cobalt-painted bathtub panel to the light aquas in the band of mosaic tiles that punctuates the white-tiled wall. Like the tiles, the toilet seat brings together both light and dark shades and adds lively pattern to the scheme.

Suite: The sink and toilet have classic Art Deco styling and traditional taps, but replacing the original toilet seat with a quirky fish-patterned design has added a touch of individuality. The bath is panelled with tongue-and-groove boards, painted in a blue that matches the shower curtain.

Radiator: The radiator provides another opportunity to add color to the room. Try to use a special radiator paint or, if you can't find one in the color you want, apply a coat of multi-surface primer followed by your chosen color in oil-based gloss or eggshell. Make sure the radiator is cold before you start painting.

Mirror: Choose a mirror with a plain wooden frame, and you can paint it to match your color scheme. Use a woodstain if you want the grain to remain visible.

BATHROOM TIP
Turn a wooden toilet seat into a work of art using colored images cut from wrapping paper or magazines. Sand the seat, brush on PVA adhesive and, when tacky, stick the images on top. Leave to dry, then apply a coat of clear varnish

The look: The best bathrooms combine function with flair, and a touch of individual style can make all the difference. In this room, classic elements, quirky accessories and theatrical color make a stimulating mix.

Color: Walls covered in deep Mediterranean blue create a dramatic atmosphere, and an electrifying contrast comes from accents of bright pink, inspired by the pink plastic bath toy. Using pink to highlight the skirting and dado rail enhances the classic flavor of the scheme. The white-painted floorboards and sheer curtains provide a touch of light relief, and the aqua green of the mirror unit also makes a fresh contrast for the dark walls. White and pink come together in the woven chair and laundry basket.

Suite: The roll-top bath is complemented by traditional taps. For an even more decorative look, paint the base of the bath in a color to match your room scheme, using water-resistant paint. This room also features a classic pedestal sink, again with traditional tap knobs.

Accessories: Don't stop at toothbrush holders and soap dishes – adding a few arty extras can make your bathroom into a place where you want to spend some time. Stamp your own style on the room with pictures or wall ornaments. Mirrors can also provide decorative opportunities – look for unusual shapes or frames, or period-style designs such as the Art Deco mirror and shelf unit above the basin.

The look: With mosaic tiles covering the walls, bath surround and floor, this bathroom is a real labor of love – the effect is easy to achieve but does take time.

Color: Pure white clears the senses to give this room its spartan charm, which is emphasized by the natural textures of the accessories. The mosaic patterning adds subtle interest to the white surfaces, and its irregular shaping gives an individual look. The blue wave adds a single splash of eye-catching color which is dramatic in its simplicity.

Tiles: Irregularly shaped mosaics can be created by smashing up ceramic wall tiles. Place a few in a thick plastic bag and secure the top. Wearing safety goggles, tap with a hammer to break the tiles. Using a craft knife, score the surface you want to cover to give a key, then draw on a design with pencil. Lay the tile pieces within your design lines and cut to shape with tile cutters if necessary. Stick them down by applying waterproof PVA glue or tile adhesive to your surface. When all the tiles have set, mix and apply waterproof grout following the maker's instructions. When dry, polish up the mosaic with a soft cloth.

Accessories: The collection of unusual accessories puts some soul into the room. The hand-crafted rosewood corner cabinet depicts the tree of life, while a pagan wand leans against the wall. The shells and driftwood scattered across the floor are natural finds picked up around the world. A candle in the corner and a sprinkling of rose petals on the water promise a magical bathtime experience.

The look: Create a rainforest in your bathroom! Lush, leafy plants, a floor strewn with logs and pebbles, and tribal masks gazing down over the bath make for a truly exotic watering-hole.

Color: Let the natural world be your guide, and base your scheme on the earthy browns and natural textures of wood and stone. White walls freshen the overall look, while the large, sand-colored floor tiles used for the bath splashback soften the contrast between light and dark. The leafy greens of the plants and the deep blues of the bath and mosaic tiles add accents of color to lift the neutral palette.

Suite: The bathtub and toilet are from a junk yard, which is a good source of cheap fittings. Dark blue paint on the base and a copper finish on the feet make the bath look as if it was made for the room, while the toilet has been given a new wooden seat. The tank and exposed pipework is boxed in with plywood and covered in varnished willow screening.

Shower: A white curtain above the unusual round shower base stops water from soaking the room. The iron shower ring, made by a local blacksmith, hangs from a hook in the ceiling.

Floor: The dark tones of the terracotta floor tiles are perfect for an exotic look. Bring the jungle theme alive with varnished tree-trunk slices and smooth pebbles arranged around the bath, plus huge potted palms which thrive in a steamy atmosphere.

The look: Minimalist chic meets classic splendour in this light-filled bathroom, where a traditional roll-top bath with gleaming silver feet takes center stage against a backdrop of pure white tiles.

Color: White equals bright, and the effect is dazzling when it is used on both walls and floor. Brick-shaped wall tiles give a less monotonous look than square ones, and painting the upper part of the walls blue provides welcome color interest. It also helps to improve the proportions of the room by appearing to lower the high ceiling. The band of mosaic tiles, repeated along the windowsill, adds an element of smart but subtle pattern to relieve the plainness of the walls.

Bathtub: The simple color scheme unites the old and new elements of the room, with the bath painted in the same bright blue as the walls, and its elaborate silver feet and traditional chrome taps echoing the sleek finish of the modern cart. Metallic paint will give a silvery finish on claw feet, but a more luxurious shine can easily be achieved using silver or aluminum leaf. This should be applied using a special glue called size, and finished with shellac varnish – ask your craft store for advice on gilding techniques.

Storage: In this pared-down scheme, a mobile storage cart takes on a multipurpose role as towel holder, mirror support and toiletry store. Most bathrooms also need cupboard space to achieve a clean, minimalist look.

Window: Wooden shutters provide a stylish window treatment with a continental or period flavor, and can be painted in any color. Solid shutters provide total privacy when closed, while louvred ones have slats that can be adjusted to let in varying degrees of light.

The look: The bold colors and textures of a lush tropical landscape mix well with 'weathered' metals to create this striking modern bathroom. Leafy green plants and wicker accessories emphasize the natural, organic look.

Color: The stunning grass green on the walls forms a vibrant contrast with the dull metals of the bath panel and candleholder, offsetting their hard-edged industrial style with energizing color. It also determines the natural theme of the scheme, which is continued with the woven textures and neutral tones of the sisal-effect flooring, wicker chair and seagrass storage basket. The deeper greens of the leafy plants bring out the tropical feel, while the towels and bath mat lift the look with accents of pale green, yellow and pink.

Metallics: The bath panels and splashback are covered in pre-weathered zinc titanium alloy, and the dramatically tall candleholder has a similar finish. The galvanized metal cabinet and plant pots balance these dark greys with their lighter color, but their matte surfaces reinforce the stark, natural feel of the look. The only real shine comes from the traditionally styled chrome-plated bath/shower nozzle.

Storage: The wall-mounted storage cabinet combines the advantages of a closed cupboard with the ability to keep items in easy view. The lockable door means that toiletries and medicines can be stored out of the reach of children, but the mesh front allows you to see at a glance what's inside.

Floor: The flooring looks like woven sisal but is in fact a realistic vinyl lookalike. While adding convincing tone and texture, it is a more practical choice for a bathroom than most genuine natural floorcoverings.

The look: Get each day off to a bright start with a blast of brilliant Caribbean color. Multicolored stripes and blocks of vivid primary hues create a fun, carnival atmosphere in this small bathroom.

Color: Hardly a color in the spectrum has been left out, but the key shades are chosen for maximum impact, with bold blue, yellow and orangey-red covering the entire room to form a vibrantly contrasting mix. Used to paint the wooden floorboards, wall panelling and bath surround, the deep blue grounds the scheme and creates a dark foil for the jazzy stripes of the toilet and rug. Yellow fills the room with Caribbean sunshine, while the blue star-stenciled ceiling suggests tropical skies. The red-painted walls and accents of sea green on the window and door frames add punch with further exotic color.

Suite: Traditionally shaped fixtures and taps complement the decorative character of the room. Painting the bath panelling blue makes it blend in with the walls and floor, while decorating the toilet has turned it into an eye-catching focal point. The multicolored stripes on its base and the spotted design on its seat were applied using enamel paints, which are available in small tins.

Accessories: The inspiration for the room scheme came from the toilet-roll holder, which was made in the West Indies from an old oil drum. Other ethnic-style accessories, such as the tribal heads on the wall and the simple metal candle sconce, enhance the dazzling Caribbean theme, while the tropical-style bath mat and fish dangling from the mobile echo the room's fun, zingy colors.

BATHROOM TIP
Some paint manufacturers offer kitchen and bathroom collections specially formulated for steamy rooms. Designed to resist moisture and inhibit mildew growth, they also give a wipe-clean finish

The look: If you want a colorful look but are short of inspiration, a fabric can make a good starting point. This palette of rainbow hues is based on colors featured in the window blind, which is framed by a dramatic curved pelmet to form the focal point of this offbeat scheme.

Color: The bathroom is one place where you can have fun with color. Melon pink walls form a vibrant contrast with shades of blue and purple, and the mix of reds and pinks jostling together below dado level makes this small bathroom anything but boring. The tiles and mirror frame have been painted to fit the scheme.

Suite: Choosing a classic white suite leaves you free to be creative with color elsewhere, and will work with any scheme if you decide to redecorate. Traditional fixtures and taps suit the decorative

mood of this room.

Tiles: Existing wall tiles can easily be painted, but you must first prepare the surface by applying tile primer or multi-surface primer. Follow this with a top coat of gloss in the color of your choice, or use special tile paints. To freshen up the grout or restore its color after painting, trace over it using a grout pen.

Window: Elaborate bathroom curtains can suffer splashes or get in the way of taps, but this more practical blind and pelmet combination offers an equally dressy alternative. While the ruched blind hangs neatly within the recess, the window is framed by a painted MDF pelmet, cut with curved corners and edged with upholstery piping. Lollipops, shells and fish ornaments glued on top complete this fun look.

BATHROOM TIP
Combining strong colors requires courage, but one way of checking out your ideas is by making a sample board. Glue paint shades, fabric swatches and other furnishing samples to a large sheet of cardboard to get an idea of how they work together

The look: Bring an aura of old-fashioned romance to your ablutions. This look combines graceful lines and classic styling with homey touches, such as plants and pictures, for a comfortably lived-in feel.

Color: A palette of airy colors evokes château-style elegance, with fresh cream and delicate eau-de-nil creating a light, feminine backdrop. The white suite and mirror surround stand out crisply against these soft colors, while the flowing transparent shower curtain emphasizes the mood of romance. The dark wood floorboards and furniture lend the room a more solidly traditional feel, and accents of red and terracotta in the soaps and tiles also strengthen the look.

Suite: The roll-top bath and generously sized basin have the classic appeal that's essential for this scheme, but it's the Victorian toilet that catches the eye. With its floral base, and a high-level tank surrounded by a rough wooden box, it adds to the air of vintage chic.

Mirror: An ornately carved surround turns a simple square mirror into a grand feature. Try making a similar surround by using plain timber to create a wide mirror frame, and then gluing on beading and decorative mouldings. When the entire surface is painted white, they will give a convincing panelled and carved effect.

Accessories: If you've space for one, a chair adds a feeling of comfort to a bathroom, and a padded seat cushion makes it look even cosier.

The look: Traditional details and distinctive accessories set within a smart but simple color scheme give this bathroom and adjoining toilet a mood of understated elegance.

Color: Smoky greys and soft neutrals make a sophisticated mix, while the wood tones of the door and bath surround add natural warmth. Instead of painting skirtings and architraves in white, choose a color that complements the wall. The beige splashback tiles also blend comfortably with the lilac-toned walls, leaving the floor to liven things up with its checkerboard of pale and dark grey squares.

Suite: The fixtures combine clean curves with classic detailing: the sink's elegant arched molding is repeated in the toilet tank, and the toilet seat matches the limed-oak-effect bathtub panelling. The etched design on the glass shower screen completes the traditional styling.

Floor: The floor design is painted on the diagonal, making the squares look like diamonds. Prepare sanded boards by applying knotting and wood primer or, if already painted or varnished, sand them to provide a key. Plan your design on graph paper before marking it on the floor. Mask off the paler squares first using low-tack tape, and fill in with two coats of floor paint. When dry, remove the tape and repeat for the darker squares. Finish with two coats of floor varnish.

Accessories: Just one unusual object can add character, and the arched mirror strikes a stylishly rustic note with its frame covered in twigs and driftwood. A collection of traditional accessories makes an interesting display above the toilet. The shelf is decorated with a fancy edging, made simply by cutting fabric to shape using pinking shears. Secure it to the shelf with upholstery tacks.

BATHROOM TIP
If you have a large family, fitting your toilet in a separate room will cut down on liness in the morning. Alternatively, you could try screening it from washing areas by building a partition wall to provide a measure of privacy

SUITES AND TAPS

AMERICAN STANDARD
Sinks, faucets and accessories
in a wide range of modern
styles.
Tel: 800 442 1902
www.americanstandard-
us.com

AQUAWORKS
Sinks and faucets, cabinets
and whirlpools.
Tel: 877 495 2111
www.aquaworks.com

BATES AND BATES
A wide collection of sinks in
metals, stone, ceramic and
stainless steel.
Tel: 800 726 7680
www.batesandbates.com

BATH DEPOT
A wide collection of sinks,
taps and toilets.
Tel: 800 769 BATH
www.bathdepot.com

BATHS.COM
Bathtubs and bathroom fixture
online. A variety of styles and
colors. Auction style.
www.baths.com

BIDET 2000
Toilets, bidets and travel
bidets. Also, sower toilets.
Tel: 877 852 2823
www.bidet-2000.com

BLANCO
Stylish German-made sinks,
taps and waste disposal units.
www.blanco-america.com

DELTA FAUCETS
Well known purveyors of sinks
and faucets with a design-
your-own-faucet option.
www.deltafaucet.com

HANSGROHE
A selecion of massaging showerheads, faucets and wall-bars.
Tel: 800 334 0455
www.hangrohe-usa.com

HOME DEPOT
Wide range of sinks, taps, cabinets and faucets for the DIY set.
Tel: 800 430 3376
www.homedepot.com

KOHLER
Wide range or sinks and faucets in the most popular styles.
www.kohler.com

KWC FAUCETS
Faucets and sinks to fit any decor.
Tel: 877 592 3287
www.kwcfaucets.com

LOWES
Wide range of sinks, taps, cabinets and faucets. Also, water heaters, pipes and tanks for the DIY set.
Tel: 800 44 LOWES
www.lowes.com

MOEN
Designer-style sinks in stainless steel and other popular material with many collections to choose from.
Tel: 800 BUY MOEN
www.moen.com

PRICE PFISTER
Ceramic and stainless steel faucets and sinks.
Tel: 800 PFAUCET
www.pricepfister.com

STONE FOREST
Handcrafted granite sinks.
Tel: 888 682 2987
www.stoneforest.com

VINTAGE TUB AND BATH
Vintage clawfoot tubs, showers, sinks and toilets.
Tel: 877 868 1369
www.vintagetub.com

WATERWORKS
Plumbing, fixtures, tubs and sinks.
Tel: 800 998 BATH

WHITEHAUS
Wide collection of sinks in metals and ceramics.
Tel: 800 527 6690
www.whitehaus.com

SHOWERS

ARTISTCRAFT
Wide selection of glass shower enclosures.
Tel: 905 847 0221
www.artistcraft.com

GEMINI
Wide range of all directional showerheads as well as designer showers and stalls.
Tel: 520 770 0667
www.geminishowers.com

HANSGROHE
A selecion of showerheads, faucets and wallbars.
Tel: 800 334 0455
www.hangrohe-usa.com

MAAX COLLECTION
Several collections of showers and bathtubs.
Tel: 800 463 6229
www.maaxcollection.com

PETERSON INDUSTRIES
High-quality shower
enclosures in stylish
contemporary shapes;
wide range of bath screens.
Tel: 800 432 8549
www.petersonindustries.com

SHOWERLUX
Wide range of shower enclosures, including some fitted
with hydrotherapy jets; baths
in some unusual shapes.
Tel: 800 257 1594
www.showerlux.net

WONDER SHOWER
Wide selection of shower-
heads and shower massagers.
Tel: 800 595 0385
www.showeringgifts.com

BROOKSTONE
Portable and waterproof space
heaters, perfect for the small
bathroom.
Tel: 800 846 3000
www.brookstone.com

HAMMACHER SCHLEMMER
A selection of fashionable
heated towel racks and
fog-free mirrors.
Tel: 800 321 1484
www.hammacher.com

HOME DEPOT
Bath fans and parts,
ventilation systems.
Tel: 800 430 3376
www.homedepot.com

MYSON TOWEL WARMERS
Towel warmers in many
shapes, styles and sizes,
including radiator models.
Tel: 800 875 7999
www.mysoninc.com

HEATING AND VENTILATION

SEARS
Natural, gas and electric
water heaters.
Tel: 800 349 4358
www.sears.com

SILVO HOME
Heated towel racks and small
bathroom heaters.
Tel: 800 331 1261
www.silvo.com

WAL-MART
Space heaters and air purifiers
for the bathroom.
Tel: 800 WALMART
www.walmart.com

LIGHTING

ALTAMIRA LIGHTING
Unique metal and resin table
and floor lamps with unique
shades and finials.
Tel: 401 245 7676
www.aliamiralighting.com

BLOOMING LIGHTS
Unique lighting with handmade metal mesh lampshades
in copper, brass, and stainless,
featuring flower shapes. All
items are made-to-order.
Tel: 800 295 0559
www.bloominglights.com

CRATE AND BARREL
Huge range of light
fixturess, from traditional
to cutting-edge.
Tel: 800 967 6696
www.crateandbarrel.com

DESIGN WITHIN REACH
Contemporary desk, floor,
and hanging lights..
Tel: 800 944 2233
www.dwr.com

IKEA
Affordable lighting, including
track and spotlight systems.
Tel: 516 681 4532
www.ikea-usa.com

LIGHTING STORE USA

All kinds of lighting fixtures and contemporary lamps. Available online only.
www.lightingstoreusa.com

RUTH'S LAMPS AND SHADES, INC.

Custom made lampshades in a variety of styles and fabrics.
Tel: 215 836 1101
www.ruthslampsandshades.com

SHADES OF LIGHT

Table and floor lamps, ceiling fixtures, sconces, chandeliers, and more.
Tel: 800 262 6612
www.shades-of-light.com

VINTAGE LIGHTING

Rewired and restored fixtures of electric, converted gas and combination lighting.
Tel: 705 742 8078
www.vintagelighting.com

FLOORING

ARMSTRONG

Linoleum and vinyl in a selection of wood and stone, smmoth or textured.
Tel: 800 233 3823
www.armstrong.com

CARPET INNOVATIONS

Sisal, coirs, wool seagrass and jute flooring.
Tel: 800 457 4457
www.carpetinnovations.com

CLASSEN

A large selection of wood laminate flooring.
Tel: 800 834 8664
www.classenusa.com

DALSOCONGOLEUM

Wood, stone and tile laminate and linoleum.
Tel: 800 274 3266
www.congoleum.com

CROSSVILLE CERAMIC

Porcelain and stone in a variety of colors and designs.
Tel: 931 484 2110
www.crossville-ceramics.com

E.Z. ORIENTAL INC.

Bamboo flooring in several finishes.
Tel: 888 395 8887
www.bamboofloor.net

HEARTWOOD PINE FLOORS
Pine floors in a variety of finishes.
Tel: 800 524 7463
www.heartwoodpine.com

JELINEK GROUP
Finished and nonfinished cork floors in several colors, tree and environment friendly.
Tel: 716 439 4644
online ordering:
www.corkstore.com

UNIVERSAL SLATE
Natural stone flooring in slate and limestone as well as mosaic tiles.
Tel: 888 677 5283
www.universalslate.com

SPLASHBACKS

ANN SACK TILES
A wide range of tiles on many colors, styles and collections.
Tel: 800 278 8453
www.annsacktile.com

BROOKS
Stainless steel and copper splashbacks and counters, sinks and vents. Brass and wood also available.
Tel: 800 244 5432
www.brookswood.com

COLD SPRING GRANITE
Granite countertops for the kitchen and bathroom.
Tel: 320 685 3621
www.coldspringgranite.com

DECO ART TILE
A wide selection of colors and patters, with many different collections to fit any decor.
Tel: 800 331 8509
www.decoarttile.com

DECORATIVE CERAMIC TILE
A wide selection of handcrafted ceramic tiles and wood frame designs.
Tel: 630 924 5861
www.decorativeceramictile.com

FIREWORKS TILES
A variety of handpainted and handcrafted ceramic tiles for counters and splashbacks.
Tel: 540 675 9905
www.fireworktiles.com

FRIGO DESIGN
Copper and stainless steel, quilted patterns. Available in metal alloy.
Tel: 800 836 8746
www.frigodesign.com

TILE FANTASTIC
Ceramic clay bisque tile (red and white), glass and mosaic tiles. Floor tiling also available.
Tel: 408 371 6247
www. tilefantastic.com

ACE HARDWARE
Paint and paint supplies including stencils and painting advice..
Tel: 630 990 6600
www.acehardware.com

BENJAMIN MOORE
A wide selection of indoor and outdoor paints and stains in many colors and finishes.
Tel: 800 344 0400
www.benjaminmoore.com

BREWSTER WALLCOVERING COMPANY
They carry a wide selection of contemporary wallcoverings, borders and fabrics.
Tel: 800 366 1700
www.brewsterwallcovering.com

DUTCH BOY
Well-known for their interior and exterior paint, this company offers a wide variety of colors and finishes.
Tel: 800 828 5669
www.dutchboy.com

GLIDDEN
Well-known for their paint, this company offers a wide variety of colors and finishes.
Tel: 800 GLIDDEN
www.gliddenpaint.com

HOME DEPOT
Major retail outlet for all your home improvement needs, they carry many designer paint brands as well as lower priced ones.
Tel: 800 430 3376
www.homedepot.com

PAINTS AND WALLPAPERS

LOWES
Popular retail outlet for all your home improvement needs, they also carry paint brands.
Tel: 800 44 LOWES
www.lowes.com

SHERWIN WILLIAMS
Popular paint store carries many brands, finishes and colors, including Martha Stewart.
www.sherwinwilliams.com

DECORATIVE EFFECTS

BJS CRAFT SUPPLIES
Beads, chimes, craft kits and general art supplies.
Tel: 361 286 3719
www.bjscraftsupplies.com

DESIGNER STENCILS
Stencils in numerous designs and shpes for all sized needs.
Tel:800 822 STEN

DICK BLICK
All art supplies available, including mosaic tiles, frames and canvases.
Tel: 800 828 4548
www.dickblick.com

ETCHWORLD
Supplies for the etching, painting and engraving of glass.
Tel: 800 872 3485
www.etchworld.com

FAUX STORE
Faux finishes, custom imprints and more.
Tel: 800 270 8871
www.fauxstore.com

FISCHER AND JIROUCH
Hand carved molding and mantels in many styles.
Tel: 216 361 0650
www.fischerandjirouch.com

GODDESS DESIGNS
Stamps, stencils and art supplies in a huge range of designs.
www.goddessdesigns.com

PARAMOUNT WIRE COMPANY
Artists wire, copper wire and craft wire to create your own bathroom decor.
Tel: 973 672 0500
www.parawire.com

PLAID
Supplies for fabric painting,
stenciling, mosaic tiling
and more.
Tel: 800 842 4197
www.plaid.com

BED BATH AND BEYOND
Window hardware, curtain
panels, sheers, and bed
canopies.
Tel: 800 GO BEYOND
www.bedbathandbeyond.com

HUNTER DOUGLAS
Vertical and horizontal
blinds in many styles,
colors and materials.
Tel: 800 937 7895
www.hunterdouglas.com

KESTREL
Interior and exterior wooden
shutters and blinds. Also carry
wooden hurrican shutters.
Tel: 800 494 4321
www.diyshutters.com

LEVOLOR
A wide range ofwindow
shades, mini-blinds, vertical
blinds and other window
treatments in a wide range
of materials.
www.levolor.com

NORTHERN BLINDS
Wood and faux wood blinds,
roller curtains, woven shad-
ings.
Tel: 877 861 5023
www.northernblinds.com

RESTORATION HARDWARE
Lighting solutions for every
room and every decor.
Tel: 800 762 1005
www.restorationhardware.com

RUE DE FRANCE
Windor decor with a French
country theme.
www.ruedefrance.com

WINDOW TREATMENTS

STORAGE AND ACCESSORIES

SMITH AND NOBLE
Wood blinds, Durawood blinds, natural Roman shades and shutters and much more.
Tel: 800 560 0027
www.smithandnoble.com

BANANA REPUBLIC
The popular clothier brings its elegance and style to the bath.
Tel: 888 277 8953
www.bananarepublic.com

BED BATH AND BEYOND
Towels, bathmats and toothbrush holders. All your bathrrom needs in popular styles and colors.
Tel: 800 GO BEYOND
www.bedbathandbeyond.com

BLOOMINGDALES
Towels, bathrobes and bedroom slippers.
Tel: 800 472 0788
www.bloomingdales.com

CONCINNITY
Towel racks, glass and metal storage shelves and mirrors.
Tel: 800 356 9993
www.concinnity-usa.com

SPIEGEL
Ready-made curtain panels, sheers and toppers, in some pretty designs.
Tel: 800 527 1577
www.spiegel.com

CRATE AND BARREL
Towel racks, toothbrush holders, storage and more.
Tel: 800 967 6696
www.crateandbarrel.com

FRONT GATE
Bath towels in many hues, toothbrush holders, towel racks and other bathroom accessories.
Tel: 800 626 6488
www.frontgate.com

HAMMACHER SCHLEMMER
Anti-microbial shower curtains, standing and hangin towel racks and other bathroom needs.
Tel: 800 321 1484
www.hammacher.com

IKEA

Freestanding storage units
and wall-mounted fittings
in a range of finishes, from
country pine to modern
metal and glass.
Tel: 516 681 4532
www.ikea-usa.com

JC PENNEY

Towels, shower curtains, shower caddies, shelves and more.
Tel: 800 222 6161
www.jcpenney.com

KMART

The colorful Martha Stewart
line of bath towels, bathmats
and other bathroom needs.
Tel: 800 24 KMART
www.bluelight.com

LINENS'N THINGS

Affordable brand name towels
and other bath products.
Tel: 866 568 7378
www.lnt.com

MACYS

Bathrobes and bath towels
as well as slippers and
toothbrush holders.
Tel: 800 BUY MACY
www.macys.com

THE NATURAL

A collection of brass and iron
towel racks and other bathroom fixtures.
Tel: 888 253 6466
www.widerview.com

PLOW AND HEARTH

Country-style accents for
the bathroom.
Tel: 800 494 7544
www.plowhearth.com

RESTORATION HARDWARE

Towel racks, toilet paper
holders and other bathroom
supplies.
Tel: 800 762 1005
www.restorationhardware.com

SILVO HOME

Medicine cabinets, shower
caddies, towel racks and more.
Tel: 800 331 1261
www.silvo.com

SMEDBO

Metal and wall mounted towel
and bathrobe racks.
Tel: 847 615 0000
www.smedco.se/us

SPIEGEL

Bathware, towels and
bathrobes all in one
convenient place.
Tel: 800 527 1577
www.spiegel.com

STACKS AND STACKS

Bath pillows, bathmats, shower
caddies, storage and more.
Tel: 800 761 5222
www.stacksandstacks.com

STROUDS

Towlels, bathmats, toothbrush-
holders and other bathroom
conveniences.
Tel: 800 STROUDS
www.strouds.com

TARGET

Inexpensive source for fun,
colorful bath towels, bathrobes
and other bathroom products,
even a toothbrush.
Tel: 800 800 8800
www.target.com

WALMART

Inexpensive source for fun,
colorful bath towels, bathrobes
and other bathroom products,
even a toothbrush.
Tel: 800 WALMART
www.walmart.com

ACE HARDWARE
Helpful advice for painting,
installations, working with
tools, lighting and toerh
electrical equiptment.
Tel: 630 990 6600
www.acehardware.com

BENJAMIN MOORE
Helpful tips for painting and
getting the decorative effects
you want.
Tel: 800 344 0400
www.benjaminmoore.com

BETTER HOMES AND GARDENS
Advice on decorating and
arranging all the rooms in the
house from the magazine
experts.
www.bhg.com

CONSUMER REPORTS
Reports on all major
appliances and nearly
all brand name products,
including mattresses.
www.consumerreports.org

HOME DEPOT
Helpful tips fpr paintings,
putting in bathroom fixtures
and lighting and more.
Tel: 800 430 3376
www.homedepot.com

KOHLER
Tips and advice on installation
as well as finding the right
bathroom suite for your home.
www.kohler.com

**STENCIL ARTISANS
LEAGUE, INC.**
Helpful stencil tips, where to
find the best designs and more.
Tel: 505 865 9119
www.sali.com